The Indian Wars

by
Duane R. Lund, Ph.D.

Distributed by
Adventure Publications, Inc.
P.O. Box 269
Cambridge, Minnesota 55008

ISBN 1-885061-09-9

THE INDIAN WARS

First Printing, 1995
Second Printing, 1996

Printed in the United States of America
by
Nordell Graphic Communications, Inc.
Staples, Minnesota 56479

DEDICATION

To Justice. May an understanding of historic conflict between Native American tribes and between Native Americans and whites contribute to wise and fair resolutions of those conflicts which continue.

May collaborative leadership resolve conflict before it escalates.

May we work together for quality of life and opportunities for all, regardless of color or culture.

TABLE OF CONTENTS

CHAPTER I

PREHISTORIC CONFLICT

Ever since the last glacier receded across this North American heartland between eight and ten thousand years ago, humankind has been struggling for possession of the land. Only in the last 100 years has the conflict been economic and political rather than violent. For more than 100 centuries the soil was stained by the blood and tears of those who fought to possess it.

It is truly hard to believe that these pines and prairies were once covered by glaciers more than one mile thick! There was probably no visible life of any kind on or under the compacted ice and snow. Archeologists believe that the first humans to arrive in the area followed the last glacier[1] as it melted and receded north. The geography was carved out as the glacier moved, grinding boulder against boulder - gouging out the hills and valleys of the landscape. Towards the end, the meltdown was quite rapid and the huge volume of water not only filled the low spots, forming lakes, but also spawned torrential rivers which carved deep channels. The impressive gorges found along the Minnesota and Mississippi Rivers were formed by the gigantic Glacial River Warren.[2]

Some of the lakes formed were originally huge. There were not only the Great Lakes, but there was also gigantic Lake Agassiz which included the present day Red River Valley, the Red Lakes, the Lake of the Woods, Lake Winnipeg, Lake Manitoba, and all the smaller lakes in-between. These lakes were probably reduced to their present shapes about 2000 B.C. Thus it took several thousands of years for Lake Agassiz to drain down to those levels. The drying-up process was apparently in stages because ridges which mark the beaches of the receding lake may be seen today from the air or even from some of the highways in the region. Archeologists have discovered village sites on these beaches which would indicate that the earliest people followed the lake north as it dried up.

We know that the first humans to live in the area were contemporary with the animal life of the Ice Age. Ancient burial mounds have been explored which contained ornaments, pottery, tools and weapons made of stone and bone. Some of these artifacts were made of live ivory[3] from the enormous tusks of the woolly mammoth. Since these people were the first inhabitants, at least they did not have to conquer some other tribe in order to move in. They no doubt, however, had their hands full just managing to survive in the hostile environment.

The animal and bird life was very different than today. Not only did the woolly mammoth roam the area but there were varieties of beaver and bison far larger than the animals we now know. In fact, there were differences even as recently as the coming of the French to this part of North America in the 1600's. Caribou were common then and there were more moose, elk and bear than deer. Passenger pigeons were so numerous it was said that migrating flocks darkened the sky. Today they are extinct.

If archeologists are correct in their conclusion that the last of the glaciers receded between eight and ten thousand years ago, then we can conclude that humans have been in this area a very long time indeed. Perhaps we can better comprehend just how long if we understand that Europeans have been here less than five percent of that human history. Even the Dakota Sioux, the first tribe to come into the area that is still here, did not arrive until about 1000 A.D., which represents only about 10 percent of human occupation. Compared to the Dakota Sioux, the Ojibwe were really "Johnnies-come-lately", arriving in the 1600's along with the whites. The Ojibwe pushed the Dakota Sioux out of the woodlands of what is now Minnesota and Wisconsin by 1739.

So where did the first inhabitants of this area come from anyway? Archeologists believe they were descendants of migrants from Asia who had originally crossed to North America by way of the Bering Straits[4] to Alaska. It is thought they then moved down the west coast. From there they migrated east across the continent. One has to wonder why they would leave the pleasant and relatively mild climate of what is now Washington, Oregon and California to travel east over a mountain range, across deep rivers, and through a hostile wilderness just to chase a glacier north into the land of woolly mammoths, short face bears and saber-toothed tigers! Were they just curious and wanting to explore? Was there a food shortage? Were they looking for an easier way of life? Or had the west coast become crowded enough so that they decided to find a safer place free from the dangers of attack? The author's guess is "all of the above", with the latter perhaps being the most important reason. Food may have been a problem. We know from oral histories that as recently as a few hundred years ago some tribes became nomadic because of food shortages caused by droughts or because animals upon which they were dependent for food and clothing were becoming scarce. In the 1700's the French recorded times when big game and fur bearers died off from disease and/or over-hunting. So it is possible the tribes moved because of a shortage of food.

It is believed that these earliest Native Americans came from a variety of places in Asia[5] because of significant differences among the tribes. Their languages are different; even the root words of tribes that have been in contact for hundreds of years are different. There are also differences in physical appearance. The Dakota Sioux, for example, are relatively tall, while the Ojibwe are of a stockier build. There are also differences in culture—including religion, food, pottery, implements, games, etc.

Yet, in spite of these differences, these first peoples had much in common and, indeed, much in common with us. After all, they were human beings, and like us they surely worked for a living, built shelters, clothed themselves according to current styles, played games, developed friendships, laughed, loved, fought, cried, worshipped, and cared for their children. They probably lived as families and had special ties with the clans to whom they were related.

We will never know how long these first people lived in peace or whether some disease claimed them before some other tribe destroyed them, pushed them out, or assimilated them. Surely North America was relatively sparsely populated in those first thousands of years and there should have been room for all. Yet, human nature, being what it is, there were no doubt conflicts. "The grass was always greener" elsewhere then, just as it is today and one tribe would no doubt covet another's territory. In the case of America's heartland there was a lot to covet. The area had both prairie and woodlands where all kinds of animals and birds could be found. Of course, that assumes similarity to the flora and fauna of recorded time. The lakes and streams were probably full of fish.

We do know there was considerable conflict in prehistoric times because large numbers of projectile heads have been found in areas where neither oral nor recorded history tells of battles. For example, the author recalls as a child visiting several times in a farmhouse east of Lake Edward (north of Brainerd) where the farmer had filled several glass jars with arrowheads his plow had turned up in his fields. Yet, there is no known battle that took place there.

Many islands of our larger lakes are excellent places to find projectile heads, particularly just after ice-out or after a heavy rain. We know from oral history that islands were the last homes of the Dakota Sioux and the first homes of the conquering Ojibwe in the 1700s (because they were easier to defend) and so they were the scenes of much fighting and therefore some of these arrowheads were possibly from those battles. Because the tribes did have muzzleloaders at that time, it is likely that many of these artifacts are prehistoric. Surely spears were not effective weapons against bows and guns in 18th century battles, and yet spearheads are occasionally found.[6]

It is not surprising that the farther back in time we go the more difficult it is to find artifacts of those earliest cultures. We do have, however, considerable information about a tribe of people who probably entered our woodlands about the time of Christ. They settled along the Boundary Waters, between Minnesota and Canada and buried their dead in enormous mounds. They are called "the Laurel Culture" and some of the largest mounds are located near Laurel, Minnesota.

The Laurel people may have come from the Pacific Coast or the Gulf of Mexico because shell ornaments have been found in their burial mounds which are of that origin. Their mounds are the largest found in this part of the continent; some are as high as forty feet and over 100 feet in length. There is evidence that these mounds contain the remains of several generations, indicating that these people lived here for quite some time. Other

Courtesy of the Minnesota Historical Society.

Prehistoric Mound, at Mound Park, Laurel, Minn. Height: 28 ft. Width: 115 ft. One of the largest found in Minnesota.

artifacts found in the mounds include sheet copper (probably mined on Lake Superior), decorated pieces of pottery, harpoons, and a variety of projectile heads. The abundance of arrowheads has left archeologists to speculate that these people may have introduced the bow and arrow to this region. It is also of interest that the bones were buried in bundles, indicating that the bodies were probably placed in trees or on scaffolds and allowed to decompose before burial. The marrow had been removed from some of the larger bones and the brains removed from some of the skulls shortly after death. In some cases the eye sockets had been filled with clay. Some archeologists have concluded there may have been certain cannibalistic rituals following death. The Laurel people were about the same height as we are today. That is surprising in that we know the human race has grown taller over the years. Soldiers in World War II were taller on the average than their fathers who fought in World War I. Suits of armor worn by knights in Medieval times would indicate that men were shorter in that day. Interesting that these peoples who lived 2,000 years ago were our size.

Some archeologists believe that the earliest mound builders on this part of the continent were the Hopewell Indians of what is now southern Minnesota. Other prehistoric cultures built effigy mounds shaped like animals or birds. White settlers found many of these in Minnesota when they arrived but they have long since fallen victim to the plow.

Sometime around 1000 A.D. a new people arrived in what is now northern Minnesota and Wisconsin and established what has been called the "Blackduck Culture". Whether they pushed the Laurel people out or assimilated them is not known, possibly some of each. The Blackduck people buried their dead in pits and then built mounds over the remains. Two such burial mounds, dated around 1200 A.D. and located at the mouth of the Rainy River, contained an interesting find: seven skulls — modeled and decorated with paint, as well as a variety of ornaments, pipes, shells, antlers, etc. The Blackduck Culture prevailed in the woodlands until the 1600s when they were pushed out by the Dakota Sioux. This was the first conflict between Native American tribes in this area that we can fairly accurately date.

The Blackduck Culture may have included several tribes, some of which are known today but now live in Manitoba or Ontario.

Oral history tells us that the Assiniboin were chased by their Sioux cousins, the Winnebagos, out of southern Wisconsin. It is thought the Assiniboin originally arrived in Wisconsin from the south or southwest. The Assiniboin probably were in Minnesota for a time before settling in Ontario and Manitoba. According to oral history of the Gross Ventre and the Mandans,[7] (they lived along the Missouri River in North Dakota) their forefathers previously lived in what is now Minnesota. The Gros Ventre once showed Ojibwe visitors a map drawn on birchbark which indicated they had once resided on Sandy Lake. Two Canadian Algonquin tribes, the Cree and the Ottawa, lived in northern Minnesota before the Dakota-Sioux invasion. The Monsonis (Algonquin-related) were also in the border country during this period. It is not surprising that many of the artifacts that have been found in this region are from the Blackduck Culture. It is believed, for example, that the paintings still visible on the rock cliffs of the Boundary Waters and the Lake of the Woods were the works of the Blackduck Indians.

The Mandans are a particularly interesting people in that they were light complected and some had blond or red hair and blue eyes. Other tribes and early white visitors, such as the La Verendryes, concluded they were of European origin or at least had assimilated whites. They even lived in walled villages, some with moats. The houses were arranged as though on streets. According to oral history, they also were Minnesotans for a time and may have been in the central lakes area. Although the Kensington Runestone, which tells the story of Vikings in the Alexandria area (found in the year 1898), has not been accepted as valid by many historians, it is a remarkable coincidence, if nothing else, that this tribe with European blood at one time probably lived in or near that area.

Other artifacts left behind by the Blackduck Culture include pots and a great abundance of pot fragments. Most of the woodland tribes had elongated pots, in contrast to the rounder pots of the prairie Indians, such as the Dakota Sioux. One tribe that lived on Leech Lake for a time decorated the lip of the pot, possibly to bless the foods or liquids as they were poured from the container. This is also a characteristic of a prehistoric tribe of present-day Illinois. They may have been the same people.

The various artifacts tell us that many different tribes lived in the woodland area over time. We really don't know if some of these different tribes were there at the same time, or if each succeeding invasion pushed the inhabitants north or west. As we have said, we do know from the numerous projectile heads[8] found in certain locations that these prehistoric woodland cultures had many battles. We will never know the details — how large the competing war parties; the ebb and flow of the battle, as first one force would have the advantage and then the other; the bloody hand to hand combat; the cries of the wounded; the scattered lifeless bodies across the battlefield when it was all over; or the grief of surviving loved ones. Maybe it is just as well we do not know.

But this we do know: the earliest oral histories of this part of the continent tell of Native American tribes waging war against each other and the victors occupying the area as the vanquished moved out — usually migrating farther north.

[1] There were probably four glaciers in all, the last receding eight to ten thousand years ago.

[2] For further information, consult *The Historic Upper Mississippi* by this author.

[3] Ivory from the tusks of animals recently killed.

[4] The land masses of North America and Asia are believed to have been joined together at one time.

[5] A small minority of historians speculate that a single tribe may have crossed over from Asia and that the language and other cultural differences came from separation and the passage of thousands of years of time. Others believe the various groups came from as far away as the Mideast and may be some of the lost tribes of Israel. Recent findings indicate at least two major migrations from different origins in Asia.

[6] French explorers did report a few spears in use by Native Americans in that day, however.

[7] For more information about the Mandans, consult *The Lake of the Woods, Vol. II, Earliest Accounts,* by this author.

[8] Far more in certain locations than can be attributed to hunting.

CHAPTER II

THE ARRIVAL OF THE DAKOTA SIOUX

As the Blackduck Culture moved into the northern Minnesota, Wisconsin, and northwest Ontario woodlands sometime around 1000 A.D., another people, known as the "Mississippi Culture", arrived in the prairie areas of what is now southern and western Wisconsin, Minnesota and the Dakotas. Whether the Blackduck peoples had been driven into the woodlands by the incoming Mississippi people or whether they were living there by choice, we really don't know.

It is thought the Mississippi people came up along the river from areas farther south and west. Among them, and probably dominant, were members of the Sioux Nation, which included the following tribes:

Dakota or Lakota (with seven councils)
    Sisseton
    Teton
    Yankton
    Yanktonai
    Wahpeton
    Wahpakute
    Mdewakanton
Iowa
Oto
Missouri
Omaha
Osage

Ponca
Hidatsa
Crow
Mandan
Assiniboin
Winnebago

Although several of these tribes may have occupied or passed through the area with which we are concerned at some time or other, it was the Dakota Sioux who were here and in control by the time the French explorers (mostly French-Canadian) arrived in the 1600s. By then, the Assiniboin were in Canada (southern Manitoba and western Ontario), the Winnebago in Wisconsin, the Hidatsa, Crow and Mandans to the west (in the Dakotas), and the others to the south (Oto, Ponca, Osage, Omaha, Iowa and the Missouris).

There is speculation that the Ojibwe may have lived in the Minnesota woodlands at some previous time, but by 1000 A.D. they were in the east - including parts of what is now New York, Pennsylvania, New England, Southeastern Canada and even along the Atlantic Ocean. Later they would be pushed back farther west by the Iroquois, behind the Appalachian Mountains.

The Dakota Sioux differed in several ways from the woodland Indians. Whereas the people of the woodlands were primarily hunters, fishermen and gatherers, the plains Indians learned the skills of agriculture, growing vegetables such as maize (corn), sunflowers, squash and pumpkins. Of course they also fished and hunted. Since the prairies had few trees, the Dakota Sioux depended more on animal skins than on wood or bark to cover their boats and homes. Their dwellings were usually cone-shaped (tepees). In winter, the skins were double-layered with air space in between for insulation. Some of the less nomadic tribes, however, built earthen dwellings.

The prairie peoples constructed their boats by stretching hides over a wooden frame, or, when big trees were available, made dugouts.

Because of the importance of the maize crop and because corn would not grow in the north, the Dakotas were apparently content for hundreds of years to stay south of an imaginary line between the present-day Twin Cities and Lake Traverse.

Courtesy of the North Dakota Historical Society.

Bull-boats used by Indians of the plains. A wood frame was covered by animal skins.

The buffalo was the most important animal to the prairie people. It not only supplied meat but also the hides were used as robes, for bedding, and, as we have said, to make boats and walls for tepees. Even the dried manure (called buffalo chips) served as fuel, particularly in areas where firewood was in short supply.

Meat of various kinds was kept from spoiling by cutting it into thin strips and drying it slowly by a fire (jerky). The smoking of meat is thought to have developed later, perhaps as recently as the time of the arrival of the first whites.

The Dakota Sioux also preserved food by manufacturing pemican. It was made of dried and powdered buffalo meat, flavored with berries and preserved in melted fat — squeezed into cleaned intestines or small, whole animal skins. Pemican proved to be a valuable trade item with other tribes and with the whites. Traders often negotiated for huge quantities. Minnesota's Senator Rice, while at the Crow Wing trading post, recorded the purchase of "several thousands of pounds" at one time. Pemican was regularly traded for or purchased by the U.S. military. There was even some experimentation with pemican as a survival food for troops during World Wars I and II.

The Dakota Sioux, as all Native American peoples, were deeply religious. They believed in a Supreme Being or Great Spirit and in life after death — the quality of which depended upon their behavior during life here on earth. Their faith called for such virtues as patience, truth and honesty. They also believed in a hell. A multitude of lesser gods or spirits were recognized — both good and bad — and were called "waken" (sometimes spelled "wakon").

Medicine men were both priests and healers. When herbs or other medicines did not work they exorcised evil spirits. They practiced the "laying on of hands" to invoke a blessing.

The help of the gods was sought before each serious endeavor, whether it be waging war, hunting or whatever.

Dances often included a religious or other serious purpose and were not performed only as entertainment.

In recent years there has been a revival among the Dakota Sioux of their original religious beliefs. Some Indians hold to both the Christian faith and their traditional beliefs. In fact, some of the oral tradition of Native American people is so similar to the stories of the Old Testament that some students of history (and the Mormon faith) believe that the Indians may be among the lost tribes of Israel. It is true that the syntax of Indian tongues is similar to the Hebrew.

Polygamy was permitted with the male being allowed to take as many wives as he could support. With so many people dying from disease and warfare, this was probably essential to the perpetuation of the race.

As with other societies around the world at that time, slavery was practiced. Slaves were usually girls or young women captured in battle or traded.

Smoking was not only for pleasure but also ceremonial — being used in worship and to bind friendships and agreements. The pipes were made of stone and had wooden stems. The favorite stone was quarried near present-day Pipestone, Minnesota; it was prized by tribes over a huge geographic area. Not only was it durable, but it was also colorful (red) yet relatively easy to carve. Pipes were cherished by their owners and there is a record of one Ojibwe chief, Old Sweet, who refused to participate in a conference with Zebulon Pike until his pipe had been retrieved from his home village on Red Lake where he had forgotten it. The wild tobacco plant was smoked by the prairie people — in contrast to the inner bark of some trees, like the red willow (kinnikinnick) used by the Ojibwe. There are stories of hunting parties being able to tell whether friend or foe had passed their way by the lingering smell of their particular tobacco.

As with many tribes, the Dakota Sioux prized jewelry, ornate clothing, and feathered head dress. Eagle feathers were most cherished. They also painted their bodies and faces on ceremonial occasions or in preparation for battle.

Most of the several tribes of the Sioux Nation got along well with each other, frequently intermarrying. There are, however, records of strife. As we have previously mentioned, the Winnebagos moved into what would become southern Wisconsin and drove their Assiniboin cousins into what is now Minnesota (eventually moving into Canada). Over the years the Assiniboin became allies of the Algonquin tribes (such as the Cree, Monsonis and Ojibwe) and fought with them against their Sioux relatives.

The Mandans and the Gros Ventres were attacked by the Dakota Sioux in 1782 at the time of the great smallpox plague. Already weakened by disease and depleted of many warriors who had succumbed, they were all too easy prey.

In the minds of the early whites, the Dakota Sioux were divided into two groups — those living east of the Mississippi and those to the west. Later they were described as "the Sioux of the Prairies" and the "Sioux of the Woodlands." Those living in the woodlands were considered to be friendlier; some even called themselves the "French Sioux". Early on they were allies of the Ojibwe. The Dakota Sioux of the prairies traded with the first Ojibwe to enter the area in the late 1600s, but later the two tribes became enemies.

During the 1600s, the Dakota Sioux began moving into the woodlands. According to oral history it was a military move that pushed the remaining Blackduck tribes north; by then the people of that area were known as the Cree and Ottawa. Some of the Assiniboin may also still have been in the woodlands.

Since guns were not yet available to these Indians, the battles were fought with bows and arrows. Some of the prehistoric battle fields marked by finds of projectile heads may have been from this invasion by the Dakota Sioux. The Dakota Sioux were never able to occupy the Lake of the Woods, Rainy Lake or the Boundary Waters, but all of the woodlands south of these areas were theirs, including the Red Lakes, Leech Lake and Sandy Lake. Both the Dakota Sioux of the Prairies and the Dakota Sioux of the Woodlands sent raiding parties further north and east

Construction of birch bark canoes.

from time to time, but they were never able to establish villages. Because of these war parties the name "Sioux" is found today identifying places in the far north — such as Sioux Narrows on Lake of the Woods. The Kaministiquia River, which runs from the Boundary Waters to Thunder Bay was once known as "the Sioux Trail". The French explorers and voyageurs recorded seeing the weathered shafts of arrows protruding from a crack in the rocks on Crooked Lake of the Boundary Waters — 30 or 40 feet above water level. They said that the Ojibwe told them they were shot there by the Sioux as a warning to others and as a demonstration of their marksmanship. As we shall see in a later chapter, it was the Sioux of the Prairies who massacred the La Verendrye party on the Lake of the Woods in 1736.

As the Dakotas grew accustomed to the woodlands area, there must have been significant changes in their lifestyle. Maize would not grow in the north and was replaced by wild rice in their diet. They also learned to make sugar from the sap of the maple trees. Tepees were sometimes replaced by more permanent earthen dwellings. When tepees or other temporary lodges were used, they were sometimes covered with bark as well as skins.

Because of the thick, dark forests, animal life was not in abundance, especially in winter. Furthermore, heavy ice on the lakes in late winter made fishing difficult. As a result, hunting parties went west to the edge of the prairie to shoot buffalo and elk. Sometimes whole villages moved west or southwest for the winter. We know that the Ojibwe, who replaced the Dakota Sioux in the woodlands, often spent their winters on the edge of the prairie in such areas as the Long Prairie-Crow Wing River watershed.

The northern Dakota Sioux capital village was on Sandy Lake. This location gave them access to the Mississippi watershed and Lake Superior via the Savannah Portage. The southern capital village was on Mille Lacs Lake, which had access to the Mississippi by the Rum River.

Thus, when French explorers as Radisson and Groseillers (1660), Du Luth (1679) and the La Verendryes (1732) came to this part of the continent, they found the conquering Dakota Sioux solidly in control of a huge area south and west of the Boundary waters.

CHAPTER III

THE COMING
OF THE FRENCH

Who were the first whites to come to this area?

In terms of documented evidence, it was the party of Louis Joliet. This French explorer and his men (possibly including Father Marquette) reached the Mississippi by way of Lake Michigan, Green Bay, the Fox River and the Wisconsin River in 1673.

There is some evidence, however, that Radisson and Groseilliers were on Knife Lake near Mora, Minnesota, thirteen years earlier, in 1660. Their journal speaks of a meeting with Dakota Sioux Indians at that location. Indian oral history also speaks of such a meeting. The explorers' journal, however, while it may have been very exact and precise to them, is vague to us in terms of modern day names and locations.

Of course, there are legends and there is substantial evidence of whites being in this part of the continent much earlier. We have already spoken of the light-skinned Mandans in the first chapter. There is also the legend of Vikings in the Alexandria area as depicted on the Kensington Runestone. Another bit of supporting evidence of visits to the mid-continent by Vikings is a grave unearthed near Thunder Bay containing a sword, axes and the remains of either a drum or shield.

There is another story just too interesting to omit here. Peter Kalm, a Swedish traveler and author who admired and talked with Pierre La Verendrye, told about an object La Verendrye said he picked up in his travels. It was described as a rock with writing on it in an unknown language. It was reportedly about one foot in length and four or five inches wide. It was fixed on a pillar and La Verendrye's men supposedly broke it off. La Verendrye also told Kalm of other such pillars found here and there in the wilderness, but without rocks with inscriptions. The stone with writing on it was brought back east by La Verendrye and given to the Jesuits. They reportedly thought the letters to be Tartaric. Present-day language experts point out that Tartaric letters are very much like the runic letters of the early Scandinavians. Interesting! It should be noted that La Verendrye does not refer to this stone in the journals this author has read, but some of his journals are missing and the reference could be in them.

To return to the documented evidence of early whites in this area about which we are writing, we do have the following record:

Louis J. Joliet

Joliet was commissioned by Count Frontenac, the Governor of New France, to find the Mississippi River; he assumed it would lead to "the California Sea". Early Canadian explorers, including Champlain, had brought back stories of the northern part of the great river. Joliet made several ventures, and in 1673 was successful in finding the upper Mississippi River by way of Lake Michigan, Green Bay, the Fox River, and the Wisconsin River. Father Marquette was a frequent traveling companion of Joliet and is usually credited as being along on the 1673 expedition. This has not been verified, partly because Joliet lost his papers and journals when his boat capsized in the Lachine Rapids as he was returning to Montreal.

To the best of our knowledge, Joliet and his entourage were the first whites on the Upper Mississippi.

La Salle

His given name was Robert Cavelier, but he is known to us by his title, the Sier de la Salle. Born in France in 1643, he traveled to Canada at age 23. His dream was to explore the Mississippi, which he believed would lead to the Gulf of California, which was thought to be relatively close to China.

La Salle's first journey was in 1669. He was gone for two years but there is little documentation as to where he traveled. Tradition has it that he followed the Ohio River to the Mississippi.

La Salle went exploring again in 1678. One of his goals was to travel north on the Mississippi beyond the mouth of the

Wisconsin River, the northernmost point reached by Joliet and Marquette five years earlier. He chose to travel south on the river himself, but sent a party of three (Accault, Auguelle, and Hennepin) north to achieve that goal. They encountered a party of Sioux, probably somewhere near Lake Pepin, and were taken by the Indians north to their village on Mille Lacs Lake. (See reports which follow on Father Hennepin and Du Luth.)

Du Luth

In 1679, David Greysolon, the Sieur du Lhut, visited a place on Lake Superior he called Fond Du Lac, (present day Duluth-Superior), meaning "the end of the lake", and there held a conclave with Indian leaders from the Dakota Sioux, Ojibwe, Cree and Assiniboin Tribes to discuss a system for trading goods for furs. The Ojibwe, whom he had brought with him from Sault Ste. Marie, were to act as the middlemen. The system apparently worked quite well for about fifty years.

On July 2, 1679, Du Luth visited Mille Lacs Lake. He named it "Buade" (the family name of Count Frontenac) and in a proper ceremony with the Sioux as witnesses—planted the coat of arms of the King of France "in the great village of the Nadouesioux, called Izaty's, where never had a Frenchman been". "Izatys" was incorrectly copied from Du Luth's report as "Kathio". And thus the ancient capital of the Sioux people and the state park located on the village site are incorrectly identified as "Kathio". Nevertheless, Kathio is the oldest village name in Minnesota, and was likely the home of the ancestors of such great Sioux chiefs as Sitting Bull and Crazy Horse. Du Luth reported that two other Sioux villages were also located on the southwest shore of Mille Lacs at the time of his visit.

Three of Du Luth's men explored farther West—beyond Mille Lacs. No one knows how far they may have gone, but they did bring back a report that "it was only twenty days' journey from where they were" to a "great lake where water is not good to drink". They may have been referring to Great Salt Lake.

Father Hennepin

One year later, in 1680, the Sioux brought Father Hennepin[1] and his two colleagues—Michael Accault[2] (or Ako) and Antoine Auguelle—to Mille Lacs Lake as their prisoners. The three men had been sent by La Salle to explore the upper regions of the Mississippi and had arrived at Lake Pepin by way of Lake Erie,

Father Hennepin names the falls for his patron saint, St. Anthony.

Huron, and Michigan and after visiting a French fort at the site of present-day Chicago. Near Lake Pepin they encountered a large war party of Dakotas who had traveled south from their Mille Lacs area villages under the leadership of a chief named "Aquipaguetin". The chief had recently lost a son in an encounter with the Miami Indians (who headquartered around the southern end of Lake Michigan). The three whites were quickly apprehended—apparently as some sort of retribution for the lost son. It was customary for the bereaved Indian to be quite demonstrative in his mourning for the deceased, with much weeping and wailing. In this case, the chief literally wept over the heads of his captives while trying to make up his mind whether to adopt the Frenchmen as replacements for his son and other lost warriors—or kill them! In retrospect, Father Hennepin named our Lake Pepin — "The Lake of Tears". At long last the decision was made to adopt the three white men into separate Sioux families; and then began the long journey north. When the party reached the mouth of the Minnesota River, they abandoned their canoes and proceeded on foot. The march was so difficult that the explorers could not make it on their own but were often carried on the backs of the Indians—which says something about the endurance and physiques of the Dakota Sioux! Upon reaching Mille Lacs, the men were separated and went with their adoptive families. Father Hennepin wrote that he was taken to an island to live. Many have assumed that he was imprisoned[3] on Hennepin Island—the small, rocky outcropping which lies far out in the lake and towards the eastern shore—but it is more probable that his island was actually on Lake Onamia.

Hennepin was apparently well treated. He was given steam baths and massaged with wildcat oil. He was presented with "a robe made of ten large dressed beaver skins, trimmed with porcupine quills". The chief had five wives and even offered Father Hennepin the use of one or more of them for his "personal pleasure". The good father said he rejected the offer. During his short stay he was allowed to baptize a sick child (which later died) and tried to compose a dictionary of Sioux words.

The news of their capture reached Du Luth while he was on his way down the St. Croix River. He promptly left his party and hurried, bravely and dramatically, to their rescue. He overtook a Sioux hunting party on the Mississippi River and found Father Hennepin, Accault and Auguelle, still captives, but apparently on a friendly basis. Father Hennepin had even been allowed to explore downriver to see if supplies promised by La Salle had been delivered to the mouth of the Wisconsin River. Enroute he named the falls of St. Anthony.[4] Du Luth, however, insisted that the party return to Mille Lacs Lake and demanded that a council meeting be called. Indignantly, he returned the peace pipes he had received from the Dakotas earlier and lectured them severely. In September Du Luth left Mille Lacs with the three Frenchmen in tow and set out for Green Bay.

The courage of Du Luth becomes even more incredible when we realize that the Mille Lacs Lake warriors may never have seen a white man prior to his visit the previous year (with the possible exception of some who may have seen Radisson and Groseilliers twenty years earlier) and that Du Luth and his companions were a mere handful of men in the midst of an army of Dakota Sioux warriors renowned for their fighting ability and merciless treatment of their adversaries. On the other hand, up until then the white man had given the Dakota Sioux no cause to hate.

Nicolas Perrot

In 1685, Perrot was appointed Commandant of the West by the Governor General of Canada. In that same year he traveled to the Mississippi by the Fox-Wisconsin Rivers route and wintered on the Mississippi at the present site of Trempealeau, Wisconsin. In the spring, Perrot and his men traveled north to Lake Pepin and

constructed Fort St. Antoine on the east shore of the lake, near
the lower end. This was the first fort or trading post in what is
now southern Minnesota.

In the fall of 1686, Perrot was summoned back to Green Bay.
He joined Du Luth in fighting the Iroquois. In 1688, he returned
to Lake Pepin. The next year, in an official ceremony, Perrot
claimed all the area for France.

Pierre Le Sueur

Le Sueur came to Canada from France in his youth. He was
always the adventurer and we find him on Lake Pepin at Fort St.
Antoine with Perrot.

In 1693, Le Sueur was appointed Commandant at
Chequamegon by the Governor General of Canada and was
charged with the responsibility of keeping peace among the
Indian tribes.

In 1695, Le Sueur was placed in charge of Fort Isle Pel'ee
(Prairie Island) nine miles south of Hastings on the Mississippi.

In 1699 he led a party of nineteen men up the river all the way
from Biloxi. When they reached the Minnesota River, they turned
up that stream and went as far as the Mankato River (Blue
Earth), and then proceeded up that river as far as ice conditions
would permit and there built Fort L'Hullier. Le Sueur discovered
greenish-blue earth in this area and thought it to be copper ore.
He brought a large amount of the substance to Paris in 1702.
Nothing more was heard of the ore but it is probably safe to
assume it was worthless.

Du Luth, Perrot and Le Sueur all made significant and similar
impact on the area by establishing trading posts. It was also in
large measure the presence of these three men and their colleagues that helped establish the longest period of peace among
Native American tribes in this area in recorded time up to the
Civil War.

The French knew if there was fighting among the tribes there
would be little opportunity to hunt and trap; the tribes would be
too busy just staying alive or fighting over territory.

It is also interesting and significant that the French (and they
were really mostly French Canadian) and the Native Americans
had such good relationships. This was not quite so true of the
English who made contact with the northern tribes through the

Hudson's Bay Company, which was chartered by the British government in 1670 and had several trading posts on the southern shores of that bay.[5] Many historians believe this was because the English were inclined to "look down their noses" at the Indian peoples while the French considered them as equals. Evidence of the latter is that many French explorers and traders married Indian women and Indian men often referred to the French as "brothers". However, even with the French there was a tendency to think of their association with the Native Americans as a parent-child relationship. Even some of the more famous French explorers are recorded as addressing them as "children".

"Bottom line", however, the white-Indian relationship in the 1600s and 1700s was a peaceful one. It is also true that when the colonists arrived on the east coast it was mostly a peaceful and mutually supportive situation.

In Chapter VII we will explore white-Indian conflict in this part of the continent. It is true there were serious conflicts, particularly in the 1800s, but in the 1600s and the 1700s the relationships were amazingly peaceful. Part of the amazement comes from the fact that a relative handful of whites were outnumbered thousands to one.

One hypothesis for the peace was that the whites spoke of "the Great White Father" and military authority in the east who would come and work revenge if the whites were harmed. But if seeing military strength first hand did not deter the Dakota Sioux in 1862, it is not likely such fears effected the Native Americans of earlier centuries who only heard stories of the east coast and Europe.

A better hypothesis might be that there was peace because the Native Americans were treated more fairly by the early whites and because the two peoples had much to offer each other, and to gain from a peaceful relationship. The Native Americans had precious furs and the whites had trade goods that would enhance the quality of life for the native people - things like cooking utensils, steel traps, steel needles, knives, axes, guns, jewelry, cloth, etc.

The more the author has studied, the more he is convinced that Indians attacked the whites when they had been mistreated by them or other whites. Sometimes the vengeance was carried out against the wrong whites or for the wrong reasons or because of hate nurtured over time, but the direct or indirect causes of violence were often because some whites had cheated or lied or taken unfair advantage of the Native Americans. There was also the important issue of territory. At first, as we know, all of the land belonged to the original Americans. Technically, it was purchased parcel by parcel, legally, through a series of treaties between the several tribes and the Canadian and United States Governments. As payment for the land, the Indians received a cash amount, promise of future annual payments, items of clothing, tools, materials for nets, farming implements, clothing, etc.[6] In each case the treaties were signed by the chiefs of the various tribes. Although the chiefs did sign the treaties of their own free[7] will, and there are records of tribal members pressuring their leaders to sign, they really didn't have a whole lot of choice. It was pretty obvious who had the clout. And yet, one notable exception was the Red Lake band. Chief He-who-is-spoken-to refused to accept the treaty and as a result that reservation remains an independent nation.[8] Many of his people, however, did pressure him to sign. They envied the money, clothing, etc. their friends had received in neighboring villages. But the chief held firm. In later years, parcels and logging rights were sold but an area nearly the size of Rhode Island remains independent. In fact, the area has increased in size in recent years as the reservation has purchased back lands with casino earnings.

Courtesy of the Beltrami County Historical Society.

Chief May-dway-gwa-no-nind (He that is spoken to). His leadership helped make Red Lake a sovereign nation.

[1] To historians, Hennepin is a controversial figure. He is credited with authoring several works which were published and widely read in Europe. They include "Description de la Louisiana" (1683), "Nouveau Voyage" (1696), and "Nouvelle Decouverte" (1697). Much of the material was exaggerated and even not true, but defenders of the priest maintain that others made his material more exciting and more readable and that his name was merely used—particularly in the latter two works. Nevertheless, Father Hennepin made a significant contribution in his exploration and discoveries and is deserving of recognition for making much of Europe "excited" about the new world.

[2] Accault was actually the leader of the "mini-expedition" and Auguelle was his assistant.

[3] Because the men were so well treated and given considerable freedom, there is some doubt as to whether they were really held prisoner.

[4] St. Anthony Falls has moved about one mile upstream since Father Hennepin's visit.

[5] Later, competition from the North West Company and independent traders forced the H.B.C. to establish ports in Southern Canada and what is now the northern portions of the United States.

[6] See chapter VIII for excerpts from three treaties.

[7] Some present day Native Americans maintain that the chiefs didn't always understand the details of the treaties and that they sometimes signed with stipulations that certain changes be made, but they were never added in writing. Whites have responded that there were Indian advocates usually present at the signing who would not have let this happen. Wherein lies the truth? We may never know.

[8] The members of this reservation have been granted dual citizenship by Congress.

CHAPTER IV

THE
LA VERENDRYE ERA

Pierre La Verendrye was among the most significant explorers of the 1700s[1], yet, perhaps because he was French Canadian and did much of his work in what is now Canada, he has never been given proper credit in the textbooks of the United States schools. In 1729, when he began his work as commandant of a trading post where Lake Nipigon meets Lake Superior, (possibly one of the posts founded by Du Luth), Lake of the Woods and everything west was legend. When La Verendrye died, twenty years later (1749), all of the main water routes west of Lake Superior — including Lake Winnipeg, Lake Dauphin, Lake Winnipegosis, Lake Manitoba, and the Winnipeg and Saskatchewan Rivers had been explored and mapped by the explorer and his sons. In his journal, he reported seeing mountains. These may have been the Black Hills, or they could have been the Big Horns of Wyoming. La Verendrye's visit to the Mandans confirmed the legend that they were of European ancestry but he was keenly disappointed that they were not French. The explorer and his sons established Fort St. Pierre on Rainy Lake, Fort St. Charles on Lake of the Woods, Fort La Rouge on the Red River, Fort La Reine on the Assiniboin River at the present-day location of Portage La Prairies and a fort on the Vermillion River in the Boundary Waters.[2] The forts were established to promote trade and to help keep peace among the Indian tribes. None of La Verendrye's forts were ever attacked by Indians, but there were times of concern when the Dakota Sioux of the Prairies were on the warpath.

All of La Verendrye's twenty years of exploration were meticulously recorded in his almost daily journals and have been collaborated by the records of the Jesuits and by letters written by Father Alneau from Lake of the Woods to his mother and sisters in France. Although some of the journals have been lost, those which remain give us remarkable insight into the French and Indian relationships and Native American history of the first half of the 18th century. The following translations of La Verendrye's journals — all written at Fort St. Charles on the Lake of the Woods — are truly priceless. What tremendous insights they give of French-Indian relationships and the alliances and conflicts between Native American tribes.

This report, in journal form, includes all that took place at Fort St. Charles between May 27, 1733 and July 12, 1734. It is submitted to the Marquis de Beauharnois, Governor General of New France, as prepared by me, La Verendrye. It has been my honor to be under his orders to establish several forts to prepare the way to the Western Sea.

Today, May 27, 1733, I sent my nephew, the Sieur de la Jemeraye[3] my second in command, from Fort St. Charles, which is located in the southern part of Lake of the Woods at the mouth of a stream, to go to report to the Marquis de Beauharnois concerning the discoveries we have already made and the two forts we have constructed. The first is called Fort St. Pierre (also called Tecamamiouen) and the second, Fort St. Charles. Both were built for the purposes of carrying out the orders with which he has honored us. He is also to present the Governor General with a map showing the new territories discovered and the people who inhabit them.

The Marquis de Beauharnois is aware that the Sioux and the Chippewa have been carrying on war from time immemorial against the Monsoni and the Cree, and even against the Assiniboin (two tribes against three).[4] Both sides are continually organizing war parties to invade one another's territory, causing a situation which, as this journal will show, is killing each other off, hindering their hunting (and trapping) and interfering with the commerce of Canada.

The Monsoni and the Cree have divided themselves into two armies and have planned to march against the Chippewa at La Pointe and the Sioux of the Woodlands. The Monsoni, with over three hundred warriors, formed the first band with the intent of attacking the Chippewa and arrived at Fort St. Charles on June 15.

At first they hid their intention from me, for fear I would oppose their plan, and asked me for powder, ball, and tobacco so that they could attack the Sioux of the Prairies, but one of their chiefs told me the truth. So I called them all together and gave them a collar of beads in the name of our Father who had forbidden them to make war against his children, the Sioux of the Woodlands and the Chippewa; and told them that if they would obey his commands I would give them everything they asked.

They accepted the collar and promised to submit to the Father's will; however, in order to protect their territory from attack, they asked me to go with them to the St. Pierre River[5] and there join with the Cree as they had promised them they would. The Cree arrived the next day, about 500 in number, intending to march against the Sioux of the Woodlands (who were friendly to the French), but they gave up their plans in the same council and all placed themselves in submission. I was therefore obliged to give them all they asked, including powder, shot, guns, butcher knives, daggers, gunflints, awls, tobacco, etc., of which I have kept a list.

The 300 Monsoni went up the St. Pierre as far as a fork where they left their canoes, then entered the prairies where they met three men who were scouts for a party of about 100 Sioux and Chippewa. The Monsoni fired on the three, killing one and taking his scalp. The other two escaped and the 300 braves returned to me to complain that the Chippewa and the Woodland Sioux were continuing to kill them and were ignoring the will of their Father. I gave them some tobacco and told them how happy I was that they had not fired on the 100 men, and told them I knew by that action that they were true children of our Father. They returned to their families highly pleased.

The 500 Cree, after a twenty day march across the prairies, came in sight of the smoke of a village they planned to attack at sunrise (they always take the sun as a witness of their bravery), when their rear-guard was attacked by 30 Sioux of the Woodlands who had come across their trail and took them for Assiniboin. The Sioux had killed four when the whole party turned on them.

The Sioux, surprised at the number of the enemy, took flight, abandoning some of their arms in their haste to reach a patch of woods

in the middle of the prairie, where the fighting continued until night-
fall. The Cree fought in the open like brave men[6] and the Sioux hid
behind trees. The Sioux lost twelve men, not counting the wounded.

As night brought fighting to an end, the Cree chief called out,
"Who is it that is killing us?"

The Sioux replied, "The French Sioux!"

To which the Cree replied, "We are Cree who are also allies of the
French. So why are you killing us? We are brothers and children of the
same Father."

When daylight came, apologies were made on both sides. As an indi-
cation of their repentance, they mourned the dead on both sides and
left them without burial, but with their arms and equipment. Both
sides then withdrew.

The Cree, after a ten day march, arrived at Fort St. Charles on July
18 in deep sorrow over the loss of their four men, one of which was the
son of their great chief. They had five wounded. It may be noted that
when the Cree are on their way home, especially after they have been
on the warpath, they walk day and night.

September 20, 1733. A Monsoni reported to me that he had come
upon twenty Chippewa and Woodland Sioux warriors on the St. Pierre
River, who were intent upon making an attack. He complained that
these two tribes were constantly trying to kill his people and that I was
holding the Monsoni back. I then sent word to all the neighboring
Indians to be on the lookout and gave them a supply of powder, ball,
and tobacco.

On the tenth day of August, three of our canoes returned laden with
merchandise, having left here on May 27 with packages of skins for
Kaministiquia. They had met no one but saw the tracks of several men.

On the twenty-ninth of August, one hundred and fifty canoes of Cree
and Monsoni (with two or three men in each) arrived carrying meats,
moose, animal fat, bear oil, and wild rice. The men begged me to have
pity on them and give them goods on credit. After appropriate consider-
ation, I granted their request.

On December 28, four chiefs, two Cree and two Assiniboin, arrived
in the evening after the gates had been closed for the night. Two
Monsoni arrived from Fort St. Pierre at the same time. I ordered the

gates opened so as to determine the reasons for their journeys.

The first four said that they had come in behalf of six chiefs of their two tribes to ask if I would receive them as "children of our Father". They said that their villages were only a half day's journey from the fort. They begged me, should I grant their request, to send their villages tobacco and Indian corn as a sign of my goodwill.

On the morning of the 29th, I sent my son and two of my Frenchmen with the two Assiniboin chiefs back to their village with a gift of tobacco and a sack of Indian corn. (I retained the two Cree.) After a six hour journey, they found an encampment of 60 Assiniboin, 30 of their wives, and 10 Cree, awaiting my reply. One of the chiefs had gone ahead to announce the coming of the party, so as soon as they saw my son they shouted with joy and fired three volleys from their guns and those who did not have firearms launched a flight of arrows.

The two Monsoni gave me a letter from Marin Urtebise (whom I had left in charge of Fort St. Pierre) and told me that 300 warriors were singing the song of war and preparing to start out against the Woodland Sioux and the Chippewa. The letter from Urtebise said the same thing and added that they would not listen to anything. So on the same day, the 29th, I sent the two Monsoni back to Fort St. Pierre with a collar of beads and some tobacco as a symbol of my strong desire that the 300 braves stop their preparations for war until I could arrive there at the Fort. I assured them I would leave in 15 days, and wanted to sing the song of war with them, even though the weather had turned the most severe of the season. Actually, my real purpose was to prevent them from going to war.

The same day, the 29th, just as the gates were closing, two Assiniboin arrived. They had been sent by their chiefs to tell me that others of their tribe, along with my son, would be there at noon the next day.

That next day, on the 30th, the Assiniboin and Crees arrived about 2:00 p.m., and, when they saw the flag above the fort, fired three volleys. Our twenty Frenchmen in the fort fired an acknowledgment. The six chiefs, escorted by my son, entered the fort. Although we marked their encampment on our charts, no business was talked that day. We spent the time exchanging compliments and I had them served with provisions and tobacco.

A council was held on the 31st. The nephew of one of the chiefs spoke in the Cree language in behalf of the entire tribe, which he said consisted of seven villages. The smallest had about 100 lodges and the largest eight or nine hundred. He implored me to receive them all as "children of the Father" and to have pity on them in as much as they were quite destitute. He went on to say they needed such things as axes, knives, guns, kettles, etc., and that they hoped to get all these things from me if I would let them come to the fort. They brought me a bundle of beaver pelts and about 100# of animal fat. In return, I presented them with one sack of corn and sixteen fathoms of tobacco.[7]

I said, "My children, I will tell you tomorrow what my Father's orders are to me regarding you, and at that time will advise you of his will."

The Indians let out a great shout of joy and retired.

The villages from which the Indians had come were on the lower part of Lake Winnipeg. Two of the six chiefs were Cree; the others were Assiniboin. They assured me they were authorized to speak for all of their villages.

On the 1st of January, 1734, at ten o'clock in the morning, all of the Indian delegation met in council with us Frenchmen. I had ordered 30 lbs. of powder, 40 lbs. of bullets, 200 gunflints, 30 fathoms of tobacco, 20 axes, 60 knives (both large and small), 60 ramrods, 60 awls, glass beads, needles, vermillion, etc. placed in the middle of the room.

I then began to tell them that our Father, the great chief, would be glad to learn they had come to see me at Fort St. Charles. In his name I accepted them as his children. I urged them never to listen to any other word than his, which would be spoken by me or someone in my place. I urged them never to forget what I was saying to them, but to carry my words to those who were back in their villages. I told them that the French were many and that no land was unknown to them. I advised them that there was only one French chief whom all others obeyed, and that I was his spokesman. I assured them that if they would obey the Father as his children, every year he would send Frenchmen to bring such things as were necessary to satisfy their needs. And that if they were wise they would bring plenty of pelts and then all I had promised would happen to them.

They responded with joyous shouts of approval. I then gave them news from eastern Canada and even from France, as was my custom with those natives who had settled around my post. I then ordered that the pile of goods in the middle of the room be distributed to those present, except the six chiefs, whom I asked to return the next day. I also gave them some corn and fish with which to prepare a feast. Without the help of the pot, you cannot have friendship!

On the 2nd of January, the French joined me in my room as the six chiefs and their next in command returned as requested. On my orders, another huge pile of goods had been placed in the center of the room, including 12 lbs. of ball, 20 lbs. of powder, 6 axes, 6 daggers, 12 Siamese knives, 2 dozen awls, needles, beads, six flags, 24 fathoms of tobacco, six cloaks with gilded trimming, six shirts, six pairs of trousers and six pairs of leggings. I divided everything among the chiefs.

After distributing the gifts, I thanked them again and again, as was their custom, in the name of the Father for coming to see me.

"I am embarrassed," I told them, "that I do not have more to give you today. However, if you are wise, you will come back to see me with all of the people of your villages after you have been hunting and trapping so that you can have your wants supplied by the trader. Don't come with empty hands as you did this first time."

These words made them smile.

I told them that the purpose of the beaded collars was to smooth the way to my fort, and that the flags were for all to rally under and thereby declare themselves children of the French and not the English. I told them I would receive them even better next time when I saw them coming like wise people with plenty of parcels of furs.

On the evening of January 12th, 1734, three Frenchmen and four Indians arrived from Fort St. Pierre, some 60 leagues distant. They brought me a letter from Urtebise which said that a party of 300 braves were preparing to march against the Woodland Sioux as well as the Chippewa. One of the four Indians, a Monsoni chief, said that the wiser Indians did not wish to undertake such a venture without my advice, but they feared the 300 warriors would probably take off at any moment because they were under such pressure from some of the older women of the tribe who were weeping day and night and urging them to avenge the death of some of their relatives.

On the morning of the 13th of January, twelve more Cree and Monsoni arrived, begging me to send my son if I could not come myself, because time was of the essence. They supported their request with presents of a collar of beads and two robes, each made of 12 beaver skins. The robes were to be my bed and my covering on the journey to Fort St. Pierre. They also presented me with shoes and snowshoes.

My return gift included powder, ball, and tobacco. I promised I would leave in two days. I summoned the Cree together who had been living at the Fort and told them why I had to make the journey during the most severe weather of the year, all for the purpose of promoting peace. They thanked me for counciling with them and offered me any of their men I might want to accompany me. They advised me to take a firm tone with the Monsoni and said to tell them they would back me up.

On January 16, I left Fort St. Charles at 7 o'clock in the morning with my eldest son (Jean Baptiste), five Frenchmen, one Cree chief, one Monsoni chief, 14 Cree and Monsoni braves, and four women, two of which would carry my belongings. In a seven days' march, I arrived at the first lodges of the first village. I found some of the warriors here assembled. They received me well and begged me to stay with them awhile to rest from my journey. I stayed one day. We held a council and I presented the war chief with a collar of beads and six fathoms of tobacco. I requested that he and his braves go with me to Fort St. Pierre, but I did not reveal my strategy.

Towards evening three Frenchmen arrived from the fort. I sent two of them and two Indians to go to the principal chief of the district to tell him I was on my way and to send word to the 20 lodges at Monsoni at the Chaudiere Portage (about 15 leagues distant at the eastern end of Rainy Lake). I also sent two Indians to notify ten lodges to the right of the trail to the fort to advise them of my coming also. I set the council for five days hence so that everyone would have time to get there. It took two more days for me to walk the remaining distance to Fort St. Pierre.

On the 29th, at 10 o'clock in the morning, the council came together at the house of Urtebise (the commandant). As presents, I had two collars of beads, twelve fathoms of tobacco (both white and black), and one tomahawk, hidden under my beaver robe. I turned to the war chief and complained that he would even think of going to war without consulting me. I then presented him with one of the collars and half of the tobacco.

I then arose and addressed those assembled, asking them if this man was, indeed, their war chief. When they assured me that he was, I then presented him with a flag, saying, "By this flag I bind you to myself; by this collar I block your road to the Chippewa and the Woodland Sioux. I give you this tobacco for your braves so that as they smoke it they will think on and understand my words. Have you forgotten the message the Cree and the Monsoni sent to our Father and to the Sioux and Chippewa last spring? Why don't you wait for an answer? That message proposed peace; yet, you seek to cause trouble. Do you want to strike the Chippewa and the Sioux? Well, you needn't leave the fort. Here are some (and I pointed to the Frenchmen). Go ahead, you and your warriors. (He hung his head.) I pity you. I know you love war."

As I handed him the collar I added, "Come down in the spring to Fort St. Charles with all your warriors—that is on the way. If you are wise, you will follow my advice. I have nothing more to say to you."

I then turned to the Cree Chief who had accompanied me and told him to speak in the name of his tribe and make their feelings known to all assembled.

He arose, presented a collar and a fathom of tobacco to the same chief (who still kept his head down) and spoke, "My brothers, do you realize what you are about to do? The Chippewa and the Woodland Sioux are our allies and children of our same Father. How can any man (he spoke directly to the war chief) have so evil a heart as to want to kill his own relatives? Remember the message we sent to our Father. Don't make us liars! We are men who walk with our heads held high, not fearing anyone. I say that you should listen to the words of our Father who gives us wisdom and come down in the spring with all your warriors to the Lake of the Woods."

After silent deliberation, the chief arose and presented me with the beaver robe which he was wearing, and replied, "This is my word. My Father, I agree to all you ask, providing you do not prevent us from going to war (against others), and that you will let us have your son as a witness of our actions."

I then drew out the tomahawk which I had concealed under my robe, along with two fathoms of tobacco, and addressed the assembly, "I am not opposed to your going to war against the Mascoutens Pouances (Sioux of the Prairies), who are your enemies."

As I presented the hatchet to him, I sang the song of war, after which I wept for the dead.

On the 7th of May, seven Frenchmen who wintered at Fort St. Pierre arrived with nearly 400 Monsoni, armed for war. That same evening they began singing their war chant. The next day I talked with them in council. The war chief presented me with four beaver robes and a collar. Before addressing me at all—he addressed the assembly, reminding them of all that had been said and had transpired at Fort St. Pierre last winter. After his long harangue he said to me, "My Father, we have come to see you, hoping that you will have pity on us, because we have obeyed your word. Here we are at your fort; whom shall we strike?"

Without waiting for me to reply, he continued, "If you wish, I will tell you what my warriors think. It is true that I am their chief, but I am not always master of their will. If you will let your son come with us, we will go straight to wherever you tell us. But if you refuse, I cannot say whom we will attack. I have no doubt you know the thinking of our brothers, the Cree, but I cannot hide from you the fact that several of our chiefs are still bitter against the Woodland Sioux and the Chippewa. You know that some of them came into our lands before the snow fell. If they did not kill anyone, it is only because they were discovered. So, decide what you want to do."

I was agitated, I must admit, and terribly tormented by conflicting thoughts, but I put on a brave front. On the one hand, how was I to entrust my eldest son (John Baptiste) to barbarians I did not know, and whose names I did not know, to go to fight against other barbarians whom I did not know and of whose strength I knew nothing. Who could tell whether my son would ever return, or whether he would fall into the hands of the Prairie Sioux, the sworn enemies of the Cree and of the Monsoni who were asking for him?

On the other hand, were I to refuse them, there was good reason to believe they would attribute it to fear and take us French for cowards. As a result, they might shake off the French yoke, which really is for *their own best interests, but they don't fully understand this. Even though they appear to like it, they have not yet fully accepted it.*

In my dilemma, I consulted the wisest of the Frenchmen at my post and those best able to give advice. They were all of the opinion I should grant the request of the war chief and even urged me to do so. They pointed out that my son would not be the first Frenchman to go with the Indians into battle, and since he was not the leader of the party, the tribes against whom they marched could not take serious offense. Moreover, Jean Baptiste was passionately desirous of going. Several Frenchmen wanted to go with him, but I did not think it wise considering possible future repercussions (from other tribes who might see them).

Considering all these things, I decided, for the welfare of the colony, to let my son go along with the war party. I did not, however, grant their desire that he be their first chief, but, instead, allowed him to serve as their counselor and as a witness of their courage. Privately, I gave him written instructions for his behavior, including his participation in the councils customarily held each evening or even in special councils to be called by him should that become necessary. I concluded the ceremonies with public instructions to my son and passed out tobacco to all as a token of my pleasure in seeing them all.

On the 11th, the army of warriors came to take their leave of me. They told me it was their intent to go up the St. Pierre River (Warroad) and leave their canoes above a fork and then proceed by land. This was the same route the Sioux of the Prairies used to come to Lake of the Woods and Rainy Lake to attack them. They planned, they said, to meet their allies, the Assiniboin, on the prairies. I consented to everything. They told me their campaign would last two months and that when the Assiniboin had joined forces with them they would have eleven or twelve hundred braves. And so they departed.

It is thought the war party traveled to the Red Lakes where they successfully attacked some Dakota Sioux villages. These were woodland Dakotas who had been friendly to the French and the Ojibwe. Nearly all returned safely to Fort St. Charles, including Jean Baptiste. This was the beginning of the end of the relatively peaceful coexistence of the woodland tribes.

In La Verendrye's next report to Beauharnois, he picks up where he left off in his previous report:

La Verendrye's REPORT TO THE MARQUIS de BEAUHARNOIS, Governor General of Canada, taken from his daily journal.

June 2, 1736

Fort St. Charles

I have already had the honor, sir, to inform you of all that hap-pened from the time I left Montreal in June, 1735, to the 2nd of June, 1736, when the Sieur Bourassa[8] left Fort St. Charles on Lake of the Woods for Montreal. I shall now continue my journal with the same exactness in order to inform you, sir, of all that has happened since at Fort St. Charles and its satellites.

On the same day (that Bourassa left) two of my sons arrived from Fort Maurepas. As stated in my previous report to you, I had sent them there on the preceding February 27th, with two soldiers, to protect that fort. They brought me the sad news that my nephew, La Jemeraye, had died on the 10th of May at the Forche des Roseaux.[9] I have placed a cross on the map I have drawn to mark the place.

They told me that the cargo of their four canoes had been left in a cache twenty leagues from here at the Savanna Portage.

On the next day, June 3, the other three canoes arrived; they had left two men behind to guard the parcels of furs.

On the same day, I held a council to determine what we should do about our short supply of provisions, goods, and—above all—pow-der, caused by the fact the supply canoes had not arrived from Montreal. We unanimously agreed to send three well-manned canoes to Kaministiquia, and, if necessary, on the Michilimackinac to bring back those goods needed for carrying on our mission. Father Alneau requested permission to go along and asked that I assign my eldest son, John Baptiste, to direct the expedition to see to it that no time was lost along the way, either going or coming.

On June 4, I learned from one of our employees who had come from Maurepas that in the month of January a white-skinned Mandan had come disguised as an Assiniboin Indian. He asked per-mission to sleep in the fort, saying that he was not a savage like the rest. My nephew, however, being quite ill, was not notified. The man who was assigned the duty of closing the gate, either because he did not understand the language or out of carelessness, put him out that

Artist's conception of Jean Baptiste and Father Alneau leaving Fort St. Charles. (taken from "The Campion", a publication of the college by the same name) Regina, Saskatchewan.

night with the rest of the Indians. He didn't report the incident until several days after the Mandan Indian had left, a fact which I regret very much.

On the 5th of June, after an inspection of arms and the distribution of powder and ball to the twenty soldiers of the convoy, I admonished them to be on their guard against possible attack by a party of Sioux that was rumored to be on the lake. They told me not to worry and assured me they would keep a sharp lookout.

Father Alneau was in a canoe manned by six good men whom I had engaged when I was at Michilimackinac and brought back with me to accompany me in my explorations, but all carried half-loads to make possible a speedy journey. Each of the other two canoes also carried seven men. My eldest son, (John Baptiste) also went with them; I could not deny him to the Reverend Father.

On the sixth, because I was worried about the two men who had remained with the cached furs (at the Savanna portage), I sent my son with five men to look for them. I gave him orders to bring everything here that had belonged to my nephew.

On June 12th, three Monsoni arrived and told me that on the 4th Bourassa had encountered a party of Sioux of the Prairies who had robbed him but otherwise did not harm him.

On the fourteenth, I received a letter from Bourassa, written on June 6 at Fort St. Pierre, giving me the details of his capture by the Sioux some six leagues from here. He reported that he had asked the

Sioux why they had stopped him, since they were brothers and good friends. They replied that when warriors were on the march it was the custom to know no one, but that they had a grievance against the French for providing their enemies with arms with which to kill the Sioux. He reminded them that the French had given them arms as well, and so they let him go.

On the seventeenth, the Sieur le Gras arrived from Kaministiquia with two (long awaited) canoes laden with merchandise. I eagerly inquired as to news of our convoy, but he had none. On the nineteenth, I sent le Gras to follow the route our people had taken; he carried a letter I had the honor of preparing for you the previous day reporting all this. I gave him an escort of eight of our soldiers commanded by a sergeant.

On June 20th, thirty Cree arrived loaded with game they had killed. They immediately set out to join in the search; however, a strong wind the next day compelled them to give up. The following day, after trading with us, they embarked for their village.

On the same day, the 22nd, the sergeant and his men returned bringing the sad news of the massacre of the twenty-one men seven leagues from here on a little island.[10] Most of the bodies were found (all decapitated) lying in a circle, which leads me to believe they were killed while holding counsel. The heads were wrapped in beaver skins.

The sad news spread quickly and the Cree and Monsoni came from all sides to ask if it were true.

On the 26th, I ordered the rebuilding of the fort, making it so invulnerable that four men could hold it against a hundred.

On July 9, four Frenchmen arrived from Kaministiquia. They had cached eighty leagues from here their merchandise — for lack of food (for strength) and had proceeded here.

August 4th: four delegates arrived from the Cree and Monsoni. They told me that the chiefs of the two tribes had sent them for the purpose of placing me at the head of their peoples to lead them in the fall in the avenging of the death of my son and the other Frenchmen. I replied that I would have to wait for word from their Father, but when I had heard from you I would advise them accordingly. I thanked them, however, for their good intentions and for their concern with the deaths of my son and the others.

On the 6th I sent my son and eight men to bring back the goods the four Frenchmen had cached eighty leagues from here. As you can see, Monsieur, we do have our problems. They cause us both expense and a loss of time.

On August 11th, two more delegates arrived from the Monsoni and the Cree, who were busy at the time harvesting wild rice. They told me that the men, women, and children were all weeping both day and night because of the death of my son, whom both tribes had adopted as their chief. They said that they were all ready to follow me against the Sioux in taking vengeance for the loss of my son and the other Frenchmen. I gave them the same reply; that I was waiting for instructions from you. They left on the 13th, quite satisfied.

On the 18th, two Monsoni arrived and reported that as they made their way around the Lake of the Woods they had found in the southern part of the lake[11] two of the canoes (of the murdered Frenchmen). They contained the spoiled furs our men had been carrying to the East. They also found twenty Sioux canoes, fastened together by twos. They were quite bloody. They also found the limbs of dead bodies protruding out of the sand along the beach (where they had been hastily buried). Thus we know that some of the Sioux had been killed and perhaps others wounded. The third canoe was found on the island where the massacre had taken place.

On August 26, twelve Monsoni and Cree arrived from Lake Winnipeg in four canoes. They said that their two tribes had gathered at Fort Maurepas and were pleading with me to let them know if I intended to seek vengeance for the death of my son (whom they had made their chief while he was building the Fort in their country) and the other Frenchmen. They said that they had not ceased to mourn their deaths. They further stated that it was their plan to send a strong warparty against the Sioux. They would soon leave Maurepas for Fort Point of Woods,[12] where, about fifty leagues from Fort St. Charles, they would meet the Assiniboin. It was their hope that either I or one of my sons would come to lead them against the enemy. At the very least, they said, they hoped that I would send a canoe with a supply of powder, ball, and tobacco.

On September 3, I held an important council with La Colle, the principal chief of the Monsoni. He is also held in high regard by the Cree and the Assiniboin because of his wisdom and bravery. La Mikouenne, a Cree chief, was also present.

In keeping with their custom, we began by weeping for the dead.

They then proposed that several small warparties be sent against the Sioux. I reminded them that this would mean forgoing the fall hunting and the gathering of wild rice for both them and us. Nevertheless, I thanked them, and said, "My children, I cannot let you go to war until I hear from your Father. When I do, I will then contact you. Besides, you know that we are short of powder and ball because the canoes from the East have not come, so how can we go to war?"

I continued, "But I would propose that we send word to the Monsoni at Rainy Lake to form a party to go to meet the French convoy and escort them safely here, and that fifty men be kept here at Fort St. Charles now and in the future so that we will not be vulnerable to Sioux attack."

To bind them to my plan I gave a collar of beads to La Colle to be kept by the Monsoni at Fort St. Pierre and another to La Mikouenne to be kept by the Cree here at Fort St. Charles on Lake of the Woods. In addition, I promised that twenty fathoms of tobacco and a supply of powder and ball will be delivered to each tribe, every spring and fall. These, Monsieur, are the steps I have taken to guard against any future surprises. All of this was agreed to and put into effect this fall.

There were further visits by area chiefs, all urging La Verendrye to lead them against the Dakotas — both of the woodlands and the prairies. On September 15, La Verendrye made his reply, listing five reasons why he could not:

1. "Understand, my children, that the French never undertake war without consulting their Father, and then only by his order. Thus, you see, my hands are tied no matter how angry I may be.

2. I thank you for the concern you have for the death of the French, particularly for my son, who loved you very much.

3. You know that there are Frenchmen living with the Sioux (on Lake Pepin). We cannot avenge French blood by causing more French blood to be spilled. And what of your own young men? Should they escape death in the initial battle and should you be successful (against the Sioux), would they escape the retaliation by your enemies which would surely follow? I would urge La Colle, La Mikouenne, and all the chiefs to yield to my request for these very good reasons.

4. I have long desired to visit your country and Fort Maurepas and I shall surely do so next winter. Then I will advise you of the wishes of our Father.

5. Finally, no matter how much hurt I feel or how sick at heart I may be, and even though it would heal my heart and cover me with glory to be able to lead your three brave tribes with so many good warriors and experienced chiefs into battle, I am held back by all of the reasons I have given you.

La Colle, after conferring on the spot with the chiefs of the three tribes, presented me with a collar and then spoke thus in their behalf: "My Father, when you came into our land, you brought us things we needed and promised to continue doing so. For two years we lacked nothing. Now, through default by the traders, we lack everything. You forbade us to go to the British, and we obeyed you. Now if we are compelled to go there to get guns, powder, kettles, tobacco, and other things, you must only blame your own people."

"This collar is to tell you to go yourself to our Father in Montreal and tell him firsthand of our needs, that he may have pity on us. Assure him that we are his loyal children, having a French heart ever since we have known him. We give you the brother of La Mikouenne to go with you; he will speak to the Father in behalf of all three tribes. Until you return, we shall remain here with your people to protect your forts. Next spring we shall go on a campaign against the Sioux to avenge the shedding of French blood, which is our own, and to protect our children against future aggression. You will not need to have any part in it; it will be I and the other chiefs of the three tribes (who will bear the responsibility). We beg you to send word from our Father from Michilimackinac in order that we may obey and honor it."

The Cree chief, as representative of the two tribes of Fort Maurepas, then arose and said, "I thank you, my Father, for the gifts you are making to our warriors to stop them (from going to war). I will report what you have said to the men who are gathered at Point of Woods Fort as well as to all who may join them there later. However, they are so inflamed against the Sioux, I don't know whether they will listen to you. I will, nevertheless, do my best to make them understand the situation and to stop them. I will tell them that you wish to see them this winter at your fort and ask them to bring meat and fats."

As we shall see in later chapters, La Verendrye was unable to prevent his Native American friends from going to war against the Dakota Sioux. The Ojibwe remained neutral at first but they also turned against the Dakota Sioux by 1739. The Dakotas were driven from all their woodland villages.

There is so much to learn from La Verendrye's reports:

1. He and his French colleagues clearly had an excellent relationship with the woodland tribes of what is now Canada and northern Minnesota. Some even spoke of having "French hearts". Tribes were ready, even eager, to help the French avenge the loss of Jean Baptiste, Father Alneau, and the nineteen soldier-voyageurs.

2. Although the French may have considered the Native Americans as equals, both the Indians and the French seemed to assume somewhat of a child-parent relationship.

3. The French worked very hard to keep peace so that the fur trade business could continue.

4. The Ojibwe, who were still relatively few in number at this time, except around Lake Superior at places like LaPointe—were clearly allied with the Dakota Sioux of the Woodlands and had been since the arrival of Du Luth in 1679. (They did not turn against the Dakota Sioux until after the 1736 massacre of the French.)

5. Although the Cree, Monsonis and the Assiniboin respected the French request that they not fight with the Dakota Sioux friendly to the French there was no love lost towards any of the Dakota Sioux, whether of the woodlands or the prairies. After all, it was probably the Sioux of the Woodlands who had pushed these tribes out of what is now the Minnesota woodlands in the 1600s.

Although La Verendrye's journals give us significant insights into tribal relations and conflicts and the French Canadians' relationships with the Native American tribes, we must remember this was a white man's view. We have only sketchy oral histories of how the Indian peoples perceived this era.

[1] For further information about the La Verendryes, consult *Lake of the Woods, Vol. II, Earliest Accounts*, by this author.

[2] La Verendrye's journals also refer to a "Point of Woods Fort". We do not know its location.

[3] La Jemeraye had previously served in the French trading post on Lake Pepin (MN.)

[4] This verifies the Sioux-Ojibwe alliance founded by Du Luth.

[5] This refers to the Warroad River. Because Fort St. Pierre was on the Rainy River, that river was also sometimes referred to as the St. Pierre River.

[6] Europeans of that day lined up opposing each other and fought in the open.

[7] Anthony Hendry of the Hudson's Bay Co. observed that the French had the advantage of the English in every way in trading with the Indians, except that their tobacco was inferior. The French had white tobacco grown on the east coast and packaged it in 12# bales. The English had black Brazilian tobacco which was stronger and much preferred by the Indians. They mixed it with a variety of leaves and other ingredients including the bark of the red willow (Kinnikinnick) to enhance the flavor and to make it go farther.

[8] Although Bourassa served under La Verendrye, the relationship was sometimes strained. He was usually stationed at the Rainy Lake Fort or on The Vermillion River of the Boundary Waters.

[9] On the Red River. The map has been lost; the grave never located.

[10] There has long been speculation as to which island this was. A small island fitting the description others have given has been named "Massacre Island". Some Lake of the Woods Indians, at the turn of this century, reportedly said a "Holy Man" was killed here. Some historians disagree, however, and are still looking for the "real" massacre island.

[11] Muskeg Bay.

[12] Although probably built by the La Verendryes, they did not report it as being built by them. It may have been a temporary post. La Verendrye could have talked about it in his lost journals.

CHAPTER V

THE OJIBWE
ON THE MOVE

As stated earlier, it is entirely possible the Ojibwe were in the Minnesota-Wisconsin-Ontario woodlands in some prehistoric time. Ojibwe tradition has it that their early migration was led by a strange phenomenon referred to in their oral history as a gigantic white shell. Some present day tribal members believe this was a description of the last glacier — which in the distance may have had the appearance of a large white shell — and that the migration literally followed the receding glacier north.

The Ojibwe are a part of the Algonquin family of tribes:

Ojibwe[1] (Chippewa or Anishinaubay)
Ottawa
Sac
Fox
Potawatomi
Illinois
Shawnee
Miami
Kickapoo
Menominees
Cree

Ojibwe tradition holds that the tribe migrated to and lived for many generations along the east coast, including parts of New York, Pennsylvania, Southeastern Canada and New England. Sea shells have long been a part of their religious traditions, possibly because the white shell reminds them of the glacier which led them north and of the shells found in the Atlantic Ocean where they at one time lived. By the time the white colonists arrived, the Ojibwe had been pushed west of the Appalachian Mountains by their traditional enemies, the Iroquois family of tribes:

Mohawk
Oneida
Onondaga
Cayuga
Seneca

(the above five had a close alliance)

Tuscarora
Erie
Hurons

In the 17th century, as the colonies were being established, the Iroquois inhabited the coastal area west to the Appalachians; the Sioux occupied the western part of the midwest, with some tribes found farther to the south and southwest; and the Algonquins were generally in between with a few tribes as far east as New England. The individual sub-tribes were spread out within these general regions. The five tribes of the Iroquois Lodge (Oneida, Mohawk, Onondaga, Cayuga, and Seneca) were in and around what is now New York State. The Eries were along the coast; the Tuscarora to the south. The Hurons had their troubles with their Iroquois cousins and moved north. The hostility grew and a "Neutral Nation" was allowed to exist in between them as a buffer.

Among the tribes of the Sioux Nation, the Dakotas occupied present day Minnesota with the Assiniboins to the far north, the Winnebago to the east (Wisconsin), the Hidatsa, Crow, and Mandans to the west (Dakotas) and the others to south (Oto, Ponca, Osage, Omaha, Iowa, and the Missouris).

The Algonquin were generally scattered throughout the area between the Sioux and the Iroquois. The Ojibwe were by far the largest of the Algonquin tribes and for an unknown length of time they were involved in "The Three Fires Confederacy" with the Ottawa and the Potawatomi. They separated, according to Ojibwe tradition, about 400 years ago. The Ojibwe covered an area so vast (particularly after they fled from the Iroquois) that they were sometimes described as four separate groups:

(1) Southeastern Ojibwe or "Bungi" — between Lake Michigan & Lake Erie.

(2) Southwestern Ojibwe — Wisconsin, the Michigan Peninsula and later — central Minnesota.

(3) Northern Ojibwe or Salteaux — Ontario and northern Minnesota.

(4) Plains Ojibwe — Manitoba and northern North Dakota.

Although there was, no doubt, a good deal of strife over the centuries between the various tribes and sub-tribes, the first extensive (recorded) warfare was in the 1740's. Prior to that time the Indians did not have gunpowder and there seemed to be enough land with good hunting, fishing, and trapping for all. Early explorers reported considerable fighting but it was usually on a small scale and usually seasonal. During the months of good hunting and harvesting there was little time for fighting. Winter made warfare most uncomfortable and the snow made tracking much too easy to carry out revenge. Then, too, cold and famine were the greater enemies that time of year. Yet, fighting and scalp-taking were very much a way of life. A good deal of blood-shed took place over hunting grounds, wild rice beds, and even over misunderstandings growing out of inter-tribal marriages and family spats. But most fighting was localized and between neighboring tribes.

As the colonists traded their guns and powder to the Indians, the stage was being set for inter-tribal warfare far more devastating. We have already told how the Hurons split off from the Iroquois Lodge and moved farther north. The day finally came when the "Neutral Nation" in between was not a sufficient buffer to prevent the well-armed Iroquois from launching an all out attack to rid themselves once and for all of their enemies. The five Iroquois allies, armed with weapons provided by the English, Dutch, and Swedish colonists, set out to annihilate the Hurons and anyone else suspected of aligning themselves with them — including the Eries, the Neutral Nation, the eastern Algonquins, and any Frenchmen who happened to become involved. Thousands[2] were scalped and mutilated. The survivors retreated where they could — west, and thus began the migration of the Ojibwe towards their future home — the area included in our study.

The first direct contact between the Whites and the Ojibwe was probably in 1612. As explorers, accompanied by their priests, ventured westward they found the Ojibwe scattered over a large area, both north and south of Lake Superior. When missionaries arrived at Sault St. Marie in 1640, they found a sizable concentration of Ojibwe. This village grew to an estimated population of 2000 by 1680 — a virtual metropolis by the standards of the northern tribes. After 1680 the Ojibwe moved farther west and the village declined in both size and importance. A new concentration developed at La Pointe[3] (Madeline Island) at the mouth of Chequamegon Bay on Lake Superior. This new capital of the Ojibwe Nation eventually had a population of about 1,000.

The Ojibwe migration routes led both north and south of Lake Superior; the majority chose the southern route and settled in Wisconsin. Those using the northern way settled along the north shore of Lake Superior and around Rainy Lake and Lake of the Woods. Contrary to what we might expect, there was little confrontation at first between the Ojibwe and the Sioux, even though they became enemies. The basic reason was economic. The French needed the furs of the Minnesota Lake region and knew virtually none would be available if the Dakota Sioux and Ojibwe were at war. The Sioux and the Ojibwe realized too that there would be no trade items available to them if they had to spend their time defending themselves against an enemy instead of collecting furs. As stated earlier, Du Luth was the chief negotiator and architect of the peace-keeping effort. He wintered with the Ojibwe at Sault St. Marie in 1678-79 and during that time developed a good working relationship with both the French traders and the Indians. With the coming of the ice break-up in the spring, Du Luth led a band of Ojibwe to a site near the city which now bears his name, and there held a council with several tribes in an attempt to expand the fur trade industry into Minnesota and southern Ontario. At this meeting, representatives of the Dakota, Cree, and Assiniboin pledged friendship and cooperation with the French and Ojibwe. No mean accomplishment! Du Luth also used the occasion to lay claim to the entire upper Mississippi area for France. In the same year (1679), Du Luth founded a trading post at Grand Portage on Lake Superior. He also founded posts at Thunder Bay and where Lake Nipigon meets Lake Superior. From these bases he established trade with the Sioux tribes of the lake region with the Ojibwe as the middle-men. Grand Portage was destined to become the rendezvous point for the voyageurs from Montreal ("porkeaters") and those from Lake Athabasca and other western points ("men of the north"). Because it was impossible to travel all the way from Montreal to the trading posts in the west and return in a single season, a meeting place was necessary for the exchange of furs and trade goods. Grand Portage was that place. Later, when Grand Portage became a part of the United States, Fort William[4] (Thunder Bay) became the main trading post.

Trade developed rapidly. LaSalle reported in 1682 that the Ojibwe were trading with the Dakotas as far as 150 miles to the west of the Mississippi. The peaceful arrangement allowed large numbers of Ojibwe to settle in Wisconsin and along both the north and south shores of Lake Superior. But the peace was too good to last. As the Ojibwe moved closer to Sioux territory, fears and suspicions entered everyone's minds.

This, then, was the testy atmosphere Pierre La Verendrye found when he arrived on the Lake of the Woods in 1732 — as described in the last chapter. In spite of La Verendrye's valiant efforts to keep peace after the massacre of his men in 1736, fighting soon broke out. As mentioned previously, the Cree, Monsonis and the Assiniboin sent large raiding parties into what is now Minnesota.

As indicated earlier, the Ojibwe actually seemed reluctant at first to join battle. Perhaps it was because their leadership still felt a loyalty to the French and their pursuit of peace among the tribes. However, when they had once committed themselves, it was with a vengeance. The Dakota villages at Sandy Lake were among the first to fall to the Ojibwe and this site was to become the new capital for the Ojibwe Nation. Located on the watershed between Lake Superior and the Mississippi lake region at the end of the Savanna portage, it was the key to control of the entire area.

By 1739, the Dakotas had fled from their lake region strong-holds and had moved their families to the prairies and back into the southern part of the state—particularly along the Minnesota River. The once powerful Mille Lacs village of Kathio was moved to the mouth of the Rum River. But the war was by no means over. No sooner would the Sioux be driven from an area than they would plan a counterattack. If the Ojibwe or their allies moved out of an area, the Dakotas moved back. Sometimes old village sites were even resettled by the original Dakota Sioux families. Although the Dakotas had been driven from their strongholds, they certainly had not given up; nor were the Ojibwe and their allies strong enough to occupy and control the area. When villages were first established by the Ojibwe and their allies, they were often wiped out—women, children and all. All of northern Minnesota soon became a virtual "no man's land" inhabited mostly by marauding war parties. The bands were not large—usually less than 100 braves in number. From 1739 to 1766, few tried to live in the area, and all who entered did so with intent to wage war. But when the ice went out of the lakes in the spring of 1766, the Ojibwe organized an army of about 400 warriors from their villages along Lake Superior and throughout Wisconsin. When the war party left Fond du Lac, it was said that a man standing on a high hill could not see the end or the beginning of the line formed by the Indians walking in single file—as was their custom.

By mid-May, the better armed Ojibwe had met and soundly defeated a much larger "army" of Dakotas, perhaps as many as 600 braves. The Dakotas at first fell back to Leech Lake and solidified their forces. Their first strategy was to occupy the islands of the lake. If they had been content to wait it out there until reinforcements arrived, they would have been relatively safe and could have held out for some time. Overeager and overconfident, however, the Dakotas made a grave error in strategy. They divided their forces and launched three simultaneous attacks on Pembina, Rainy Lake, and Sandy Lake. They lost on all three fronts and the resultant disaster was the turning point of the war.

Cut-Foot Sioux Lake received its name as the contingent of Sioux headed for Sandy Lake encountered an army of Ojibwe on its way to Leech Lake. The Dakota Sioux were defeated but one of the dead left behind was a warrior whose feet gave the appearance of the front portions having been cut off in times past. Another version is that some of the Dakota Sioux were allowed to live but their heel tendons were first cut.

The Sioux fell back to their villages west of the Mississippi and along the Minnesota River. The Ojibwe were, for the first time, truly in control of the lake region, and a serious effort was made to settle the area. Sandy Lake continued as the headquarters for their operations, but villages soon appeared on the Red Lakes, Winnibigoshish, Cass Lake, Leech Lake, and Mille Lacs. Just as the islands of Leech Lake had been the last strongholds of the Dakotas, they became the first homes of the Ojibwe in the area. For, even though the Ojibwe had effectively defeated the Dakotas, Sioux war parties would return again and again for many years to view their old village sites, visit the burial places of their ancestors, and administer vengeance to the Ojibwe. In fact, if the Ojibwe villages had not been replenished continuously with settlers from the east, they surely would have been annihilated.

Bi-aus-wa was the legendary chief who is credited with successfully leading the Ojibwe forces against the Dakota Sioux at Sandy Lake. When the Ojibwe eventually established villages on that lake, Bi-aus-wa took the position as head chief and his village became the capital of the Ojibwe nation. He was subsequently better known for his civil leadership. He chose as his war chiefs Noka and Great Marten. They were not only responsible for defending Sandy Lake, but they also led attacks against the Dakota Sioux, now farther south, to keep them in their place. On one such raid, Noka led approximately 200 braves down the Mississippi and wiped out a Dakota Sioux village at the mouth of the Minnesota River. When the Ojibwe left the north country the ice was just out and there were no leaves on the trees. They were surprised to find the trees in full leaf farther south and for that reason gave the name "Osh-ke-bug-e-sebe" or "New Leaf River" to the stream we now call the Minnesota River.

Waub-o-jeeg I, or "White Fisher," was another important Ojibwe leader who not only drove the Sioux from the Wisconsin lake region, (Battle of St. Croix Falls) but also the Sauk and the Fox — both Algonquin tribes which had allied themselves with the Dakotas. He not only earned a reputation in Minnesota but also made the Minnesota invasion possible by securing northern Wisconsin for the Ojibwe.

These were only the beginnings. The Ojibwe and the Dakota Sioux remained at war for more than 100 years — almost up to the time of the Civil War. But before describing some of the more significant battles, let us take a closer look at the Ojibwe people.

In late March or early April, the return of the first crow caused great rejoicing because it signaled the coming of spring and the

Courtesy of the Cass County Historical Society.

The stalks of wild rice are bent over the boat and the ripe kernels are beaten from the head with a stout stick.

rising of the sap in the maple trees. Winter hunting encampments would break up. The families, relations and even whole villages would move to their traditional "sugar bush" area where they would stay until May. Permanent lodges were located at these sites. They were large, usually measuring from 10 to 20 feet wide and 25 to 40 feet long. Sometimes smaller, temporary huts were built — called "wig-wa-si-ga-mig" by the Ojibwe. Whites nicknamed them "wigwams." The trees were tapped by cutting a slash and driving a cedar splinter or carved spigot into the wood. The sap dripped off the splinter and was then collected in containers on the ground (made from birchbark). Syrup was made by boiling the sap for days over an open fire. Although the syrup was sometimes used for food, it was usually thickened by continued boiling and then when it was the right consistency, placed in a basswood trough where it was gently stirred until it became granulated, thus forming sugar.

Often times the syrup was poured into molds and allowed to harden. This "hard sugar" could be stored more conveniently for use throughout the year. One family could prepare as much as 500 pounds of maple sugar in a single season. The hard sugar was eaten as a food or confection; granulated sugar was used as a seasoning or flavoring agent; and a beverage was made by dissolving the maple sugar in water.

Spring was also the time for fishing, trapping, and hunting. In addition to using nets and traps, spawning fish were often

Courtesy of the Cass County Historical Society.

Syrup was made by boiling sap for days over an open fire.

speared at night with a birch bark or pine knot torch for light. Migratory waterfowl were again found on the Indian menu. Muskrats were easier to trap. All in all, spring was a time for both working and rejoicing. Celebrations, feasting and religious ceremonies accompanied the spring activities.

July and August were a season for berry picking. The braves may have been helpful in locating the berry patches, but the women and children did the picking. Just as today, the woodlands had an abundance of blueberries, chokecherries, pincherries, raspberries, strawberries, and cranberries (both low and high bush). Every effort was made to preserve the fruit for use later in the year. Some berries were dried whole; others were dried and then pulverized. Boiling was sometimes used, particularly with raspberries. It was also at this time that ducks and geese became quite helpless during a period of molting and young birds were taken just before they were large enough to fly. Unsportsmanlike? Not when you're talking about food for survival!

September brought the wild rice harvest and another occasion to feast and celebrate. It was perhaps even a greater time for reunions and socializing than the sugar camps. Most harvesting was done by the women, usually two to a canoe. While one paddled or poled the boat through the rice bed, the other sat in front and pulled the rice over the canoe, beating the heads with a stick — thus dislodging the mature kernels. Since all of the rice in each head did not mature at the same time, the harvesters could cover the same area several times a few days apart.

The kernels were further separated from the husks by beating or trampling and then the chaff was blown away by throwing the rice into the air on a windy day. The kernels were then parched by the fire.

Although there were few differences in how the Ojibwe and the Dakota Sioux made use of nature's bounty, in many ways the tribes were not alike. Language was perhaps the most significant difference. Even though the Algonquins and the Sioux had been neighbors for centuries, even the basic root words bore no resemblance. It is likely that the ancestors of these two tribes migrated to North America at different periods of history and from different parts of Asia. Differences in facial and other physical characteristics were accented by diverse clothing, head gear, and hair styles. Furthermore, the Sioux were of a tall but athletic build, while the Ojibwe were more stocky but sturdy. White explorers were impressed with the muscular physique of the Indians; early drawings made them look somewhat like Greek athletes!

Both tribes were very religious, but there were significant differences as well as similarities.

Both believed in a Supreme Being or Great Spirit. Both believed in a life after death (happy hunting ground). Both recognized lesser spirits — usually taken from nature. The Dakota Sioux labeled the spirits or the unknown as "waken;" the Ojibwe called them "manitou;" Religion called for such virtues as patience, truth, and honesty, but curses were called down upon enemies. Superstitions and religious legends were numerous and varied somewhat from tribe to tribe and village to village. Gods were worshipped in prayers, offerings, chants and dances. The Ojibwe, in particular, were conscientious about offering prayers whenever food was harvested or taken in a hunt. Visions and dreams were generated by fasting and meditation.

"The happy hunting ground" was a place where the Indian was free from his struggle for survival and all the necessities of life were easily attained. Chief Bemidji described the Indian's "Hell" as a place where the hungry Indian could see hundreds of walleyes through six feet of ice with no way to cut through, or a deer was always just going over the second hill as he came over the first, or he was very cold and all the wood was too wet to start a fire.

The Ojibwe had a religious-cultural hero named "Nanabozho," who created the world for the Indian and taught him about the Great Spirit and religious practices. These practices were called "Midewiwin," and they were characterized by secret ceremonies and initiations including a guardian spirit for each and a "totem" spirit for each family group or relation. The Ojibwe had about twenty totems with as many as 1,000 members in a totem family. It was taboo for members of the same totem to marry. There were a few examples of the totem practice among Sioux tribes but it is believed that these can be traced in each case to intermarriages with the Ojibwe. The totem was symbolized by a bird, animal, reptile, or fish. In addition, each Ojibwe carried a medicine bag which contained herbs and items such as shells which represented special powers and protection. The priests were called "Mides."

Polygamy was permitted by both tribes with the male taking more than one wife.

Upon death, following a ceremony and appropriate mourning,[5] bodies were sometimes bundled on scaffolds or placed in trees — particularly during the cold time of the year — and buried later. The Ojibwe traditionally buried their dead in a sitting position facing west. A long, low house-like shelter was constructed over the grave. Food was placed here along with all the deceased would need in the way of tools and weapons to help him in his journey westward "across the river" to his eternal reward. A carved or drawn symbol of the appropriate totem was often placed outside the shelter.

To continue our comparison, the basic shelters of the two tribes also developed differently. The Dakota Sioux used earthen dwellings, particularly on the prairies, while the Ojibwe used birchbark - covered lodges. While living in the wooded areas of Minnesota, the Sioux also used birchbark-covered dwellings, particularly when they were interested in portability. But hides were often substituted for birchbark, particularly during the colder months. The basic shapes of the shelters were also different; The Ojibwe preferred a dome or rounded shape to their lodges while the Dakotas chose the pointed cone-shaped tepees. Both had openings in the roof for smoke to escape from an open fire.

Both used birchbark canoes, but when the Sioux tribes first arrived in Minnesota it is believed they used dugouts and boats made of skins stretched over wood frames.

As may be expected, other differences appeared as the Dakotas retreated westward to the prairies. The canoe was replaced by the horse. Diets changed when wild rice and certain berries were no longer available. Traditionally, the Dakotas were more dependent on maize (Indian corn). No doubt this was because the Sioux tribes lived so long in warmer climates. As the Dakotas left the woodland regions they became especially dependent on the buffalo for both the meat and the hide.

The Dakota Sioux were supposedly more warlike, but the Algonquin tribes could be just as ruthless when dealing with their enemies.

Writers have led us to believe that other differences were perhaps the result of the earlier contacts of the Ojibwe with the whites. As a result, they were supposedly not only better armed than the Dakotas but also had the benefit of such traded items as blankets, steel traps, iron kettles, and steel knives.

Present day historians discount this theory and point out that the French had been trading with the Sioux since the 1600's.

We should point out that Minnesota was really rather sparsely settled in the days of Du Luth and Father Hennepin. The Minnesota Indian population today is more than twenty thousand.[6] It was very likely less than this in the 17th and 18th centuries.

It is not difficult to understand why the Ojibwe and the Dakota Sioux would fight to the death for control of this region of lakes and forests. It was a cornucopia of fish and food and provided all of the materials for transportation and shelter. But the more than 100 years of warfare which was to follow also had much to do with matters of pride and revenge. There was also possibly the hope that total victory would permit the winners to live in peace.

[1] There are several acceptable spellings of "Ojibwe", including "Ojibway", "Objiwa" (Schoolcraft's spelling) and "Ojibwey." The tribe was also called "Chippewa", perhaps a French corruption of "Ojibway." "Chippewa" often appears on treaties and other legal documents. Theories of the origin and meaning of the word include "to pucker" which could apply to the design of their moccasins or to the effect on the skins of their victims placed too close to the fire. They have sometimes called themselves "Anishinaubay".

[2] Estimates of deaths ran as high as 10,000.

[3] LaPointe was occupied by the Hurons and the Ottawas for about twenty years prior to the takeover by the Ojibwe.

[4] For further information about the major trading posts on Lake Superior, see *The North Shore of Lake Superior, Yesterday and Today*, by this author.

[5] Periods of mourning were often characterized by much crying and loud wailing.

[6] If people of less than half "Indian blood" are included, the figure is closer to 40,000.

CHAPTER VI

THE
100 YEARS WAR

We saw in the last chapter that the Cree, Monsonis and Assiniboin attacked the Dakota Sioux of the Woodlands from their territories in the Boundary Waters area, Northwest Ontario and southern Manitoba and the Ojibwe joined in shortly thereafter from their strongholds in what is now western Wisconsin. By 1739, the Dakota Sioux had been forced to flee their villages throughout the woodlands. They established their new villages farther south along the Mississippi and on the Minnesota River. Even the capital village on Mille Lacs was lost. The Dakota Sioux did not give up easily, however, and from 1739 to 1766 they continued to send raiding parties north in the hope of re-establishing their villages. The Ojibwe countered with raids on the new Dakota Sioux villages farther south along the rivers and on the prairies. At times the woodlands were a virtual "no man's land". Even the French traders no longer dared to enter the area.

As we also saw in the last chapter, the Ojibwe in 1766 marshaled a small army of braves at La Pointe and after soundly defeating the Dakota Sioux in three major battles at Pembina, Sandy Lake and Rainy Lake, began major migrations into what is now Minnesota and established their villages with substantial populations able to withstand the raids of the Dakota Sioux. Even then, however, the war continued with many raids and battles, both large and small, almost up to the time of the Civil War. In this chapter we will endeavor to tell the stories of the most significant and interesting of those conflicts.

The Conquest of Mille Lacs Lake

It is possible that this was the first major conquest of a large lake by the Ojibwe, and it may have been as early as 1739. William Warren, in his *History of the Ojibway People* records an interview he had with an old Mille Lacs Ojibwe chief (the interview took place around 1850), who related the following story:

"There was an old man residing at Fond du Lac of Lake Superior which place had at this time, already become an important village of the Ojibwe. This old man was looked upon by his people with much respect and consideration: though not a chief, he was a great hunter, and his lodge ever abounded in plenty. He belonged to the Marten Totem family. He was blessed with four sons, all of whom were full grown and likely men, "fair to look upon." They were accustomed to make frequent visits to the villages of the Dakotas, and they generally returned laden with presents, for the young women of their tribe looked on them with wishful and longing eyes.

Shortly after a quarrel about a woman had taken place, which resulted in the death of an Ojibwe, the four brothers paid the Dakotas one of their usual peaceful visits; they proceeded to their great town at Mille Lac, which was but two days from their villages. During this visit, one of the brothers was treacherously murdered, but three returned with safety to their father's wigwam.

The old man did not even complain when he heard their former enemies had sent his son to travel on the Spirit road; and shortly after, when his three surviving sons asked his permission to go again to enter the lodges of the Dakotas, he told them to go, "for probably," said he, "they have taken the life of my son through mistake." The brothers proceeded as before to Mille Lac, and on this occasion, two of them were again treacherously killed, and but one returned to the wigwam of his bereaved father. The fount of the old man's tears still did not open, though he blackened his face in mourning, and his head hung down in sorrow.

Once more his sole surviving son requested to pay the Dakotas a peace visit, that he might look on the graves of his deceased brethren. His sorrow stricken parent said to him, "go, my son, for probably they have struck your brothers through mistake." Day after day rolled over, till the time came when he had promised to return. The days, however, kept rolling on, and the young man returned not to cheer the lonely lodge of his father. A full moon passed over, and still he made not his appearance, and the old man became convinced that the Dakota had sent him to join his murdered brethren in the land of Spirits. Now, for the first time, the bereaved father began to weep, the fount of his tears welled forth bitter drops, and he mourned bitterly for his lost children.

"An Ojibwe warrior never throws away his tears," and the old man determined to have revenge. For two years he busied himself in making preparations. With the fruits of his hunts he procured ammunition and other materials for a war party. He sent his tobacco and warclub to the remotest villages of his people, detailing his wrong and inviting them to collect by a certain day at Fond du Lac, to go with him in "search for his lost children." His summons was promptly and numerously obeyed, and nearly all the men of his tribe residing on the shores of the Great Lake, collected by the appointed time at Fond du Lac. Their scalping knives had long rusted in disuse, and the warriors were eager once more to stain them with the blood of their old enemy.

Having made the customary preparations, and invoking the Great Spirit to their aid, this large war party which the old man had collected, left Fond du Lac, and followed the trail towards Mille Lac, which was then considered the strongest hold of their enemies, and where the blood which they went to revenge had been spilt. The Dakotas occupied the lake in two large villages, one being located on Cormorant point, and the other at the outlet of the lake. A few miles below this last village, they possessed another considerable village on a smaller lake, connected with Mille Lac by a portion of Rum River which runs through it. These villages consisted mostly of earthen wigwams such as are found still to be in use among the Arickarees and other tribes residing on the Upper Missouri.

The vanguard of the Ojibwe fell on the Dakotas at Cormorant point early in the morning, and such was the extent of the war party, that before the rear had arrived, the battle at this point had already ended by the almost total extermination of its inhabitants; a small remnant only, retired in their canoes to the greater village located at the entry. This, the Ojibwe attacked with all their forces; after a brave defense with their bows and barbed arrows, the Dakotas took refuge in their earthen lodges from the more deadly weapons of their enemy.

The only manner by which the Ojibwe could harass and dislodge them from these otherwise secure retreats, was to throw small bundles or bags of powder into the aperture made in the top of each, both for the purpose of giving light within, and emitting the smoke of the wigwam fire. The bundles ignited by the fire, spread death and dismay amongst the miserable beings who crowded within. Not having as yet, like the more fortunate Ojibwes, been blessed with the presence of white traders, the Dakotas were still ignorant of the nature of gunpowder, and the idea possessing their minds that their enemies were aided by spirits, they gave up the fight in despair and were easily dispatched. But a remnant retired during the darkness of night to their last remaining village on the smaller lake. Here they made their last stand, and the Ojibwes following them up, the havoc among their ranks was continued during the whole course of another day.

The next morning the Ojibwes wishing to renew the conflict, found the village evacuated by the few who had survived their victorious arms. They had fled during the night down the river in their canoes, and it became a common saying that the former dwellers of Mille Lacs became, by this three days' struggle, swept away forever from their favorite village sites."

They are believed to have settled at the mouth of the Rum River.

The Battle at the Mouth of the Crow Wing

It was 1768. The Dakota Sioux had been driven from their strongholds in northern Minnesota but had not given up. They had even been forced from their Mille Lacs Lake headquarters village when the Ojibwe blew up their earthen houses by dropping gunpowder down the smoke holes. It was from their new headquarters village at the mouth of the Rum River that a small army of about 200 braves launched a raid against the new Ojibwe capital on Sandy Lake.

At the same time, an Ojibwe war party of about seventy men moved south down the Mississippi with the Rum River village as their objective. The Dakotas proceeded up the Mississippi (but chose to take the Crow Wing cutoff), then traveled up the Gull River, across Gull, Long, and Whitefish Lakes, then up to Pine River and across a series of lakes leading to Boy River and Leech Lake—on the way to Sandy Lake (probably because there was less current to fight).Thus the two war parties did not meet on their way to their respective objectives.

Apparently the Ojibwe did not find any indication that the Dakota Sioux army had traveled up the river only days before. They were evidently totally surprised to find the Rum River village deserted, with the women and children safely protected elsewhere. Surprise turned to horror when the Ojibwe realized the possible significance of the empty village. Their worst fears were to be realized. The Dakotas had fallen on the helpless Sandy Lake village and slaughtered everyone except thirty young women whom they took captive along with an older woman to care for them. The Ojibwe wasted no time looking for the hidden Dakota Sioux women and children but hurried back up river—intent on finding a battlefield of their liking to ambush the Sioux. They reached the mouth of the Crow Wing without encountering the enemy, and here they finally discovered camp signs left by the Dakotas on their way north. They dared to go no further because they were not sure by which river the Sioux would come—the Crow Wing or the Mississippi. They quickly dug in on a bluff on the east bank of the Mississippi overlooking both rivers (where their excavations may be seen to this day as a part of Crow Wing State Park). They did not have long to wait. A scout reported that the Dakota Sioux war party was on its way down the Mississippi. They stopped across from Crow Wing Island, where they forced their captives to serve them breakfast, in full view of their loved ones who were anxiously lying in ambush.

As the story goes, the old woman whose life had been spared to care for the captives turned out to be the real heroine. She had quietly reminded her charges that there was a good chance they would meet the returning men from their village somewhere along the river. If and when this should happen, she urged the women to overturn the canoes and swim towards the rifle fire. And that is exactly what happened. The unsuspecting Dakotas were caught completely off guard and suffered heavy casualties. The Ojibwe had chosen their battleground well. Here the Mississippi narrowed and made a sharp turn, the faster current bringing the Dakota Sioux into close range, but they were not about to give up their captives or leave without a good fight. Incensed over the sudden turn of events and the fact they had been outsmarted by their captives—women at that (Indians of that time were real male chauvinists!)—they placed the Ojibwe under siege. When frontal attacks proved too costly, they crossed the river and circled behind them on land, but the Ojibwe were too well protected and continued to get the better of the battle. At last, the Dakotas decided "discretion was indeed the better part of valor" and reluctantly turned their canoes downstream—

no doubt keenly disappointed at their loss of the captives and many of their own men, and perhaps wondering about the safety of their families they had left behind—hopefully secluded and protected.

As in all wars, everyone lost something, and in this case, no one gained anything.

Battle for Control of Bay Lake

It can probably be assumed that all or nearly all major lakes in what is now Minnesota (south of the Boundary Waters) supported one or more Sioux villages in the 1600's and early 1700's. Oral tradition has it that one such encampment was on the north shore of Bay Lake (near Deerwood), one mile east of Ruttgers Resort. About the time the Ojibwe drove the Dakota Sioux from their Mille Lacs Lake villages, they also claimed nearby Bay Lake. The Ojibwe apparently liked the location of the village and settled in. During the later 1700's and early 1800's the Dakota Sioux made numerous efforts to recapture their old village sites; among them was the Bay Lake village. As the story goes, the Ojibwe village was completely annihilated. Eventually, however, the site was reclaimed by other Ojibwe.

A painting by Sarah Thorp Heald which depicts the Dakota Sioux victory, hangs in the Crow Wing County Courthouse in Brainerd. The Bay Lake village site is called "Battle Point".

A Truce

The only significant truce during the 100 Years War took place around the 1770s when the Ojibwe and the Dakota Sioux agreed to hunt and trap in peace during the winter months in the area around the Long Prairie and the Crow Wing Rivers.

These hunting grounds were so important to both the Sioux and the Ojibwe that when neither was able to conclusively drive the other from it, a winter truce was negotiated several years running. Prior to this time, a hunter might very well return to his camp at night with a scalp or two hanging from his belt as well as furs taken during the day. The truce also made it possible to take the entire family on the winter hunt.

So good was the hunting that the Ojibwe came from as far away as Leech and Sandy Lake; these villages retained a close relationship over the years and it was their custom to rendezvous at Gull Lake or the mouth of the Crow Wing on their way to the winter hunting grounds. The virgin pine forests of the north were not good habitat for wildlife because insufficient light could filter through to nourish the undergrowth which provides food for both birds and animals. The Sioux came from as far away as the prairies of present day North and South Dakota, and included the Wahpetons and Sissetons as well as other Dakota bands.

The Ojibwe bands often traveled up the Long Prairie and Crow Wing Rivers. They were especially attracted by the herds of buffalo that grazed in the area. The Sioux were usually there first and already settled in their hide-covered tepees. After warring back and forth all summer, the only way the Ojibwe could be certain the winter truce would again be in effect was to directly approach the Sioux village and offer to smoke the pipe of peace. Dressed for the occasion and well-armed, a vanguard — not so large as to be threatening but not so small as to be easy prey — would march right into the Sioux village. The bearer of the peace pipe and the banner carriers led the procession. The customary response of the Sioux was to welcome the Ojibwe with a volley of rifle fire. Sometimes the singing bullets were so near the ears of the visitors that it seemed the "name of the game" was to come as close as possible without scoring! Once it was clear that a truce was desired, the Ojibwe were welcomed into the lodges of the Sioux where they smoked the peace pipe and feasted on the best available food — sometimes literally beneath the scalps of their fellow tribesmen which may have been taken as recently as the past summer and now hung suspended from the lodge poles. The Ojibwe had a word for this ceremony; they called it "Pin-dig-u-daud-e-win," which is translated, "to enter into one another's lodges."

An interesting custom during these periods of truce was for warriors to adopt "brothers" from among the traditional enemies of the other tribes. Often they were considered as replacements for special friends or brothers lost in battle. There are many tales of adopted brothers being spared during subsequent raids or battles. It is told that the relationships between the two tribes sometimes became so friendly that there was intermarrying and even the exchanging of wives.

The End of the Truce - Chief Yellow Hair's Revenge

Chief Flat Mouth of Leech Lake may have been the most able and significant leader of the Ojibwe in the 1800s. We will speak more of him shortly. His father, Wa-son-aun-e-qua or "Yellow Hair" however, was somewhat of a scoundrel. According to Flat Mouth, Chief Yellow Hair did not inherit his title, but achieved his leadership role through a remarkable knowledge of medicines, including poisons. It is said that his enemies lost their lives in a mysterious and unaccountable manner. His own son called him "vindictive" and "revengeful" and said that he retaliated against his enemies two-fold. It is likely that Yellow Hair was a follower of a well known false prophet or "Shamono" of that day. This medicine man turned witch doctor garnered a tremendous following among the Ojibwe and persuaded them to forsake their traditional Midewiwin religion. He claimed to have a new revelation from the Great Spirit and urged all to throw away their little medicine bags and follow him. A religious rally of sorts was held at the location of present day Detroit. However, when it was discovered he could not raise the dead some of his followers had brought to him and when he was found hiding in a hollow tree when he was supposed to be in heaven conferring with the Great Spirit, his disciples (including Flat Mouth) deserted him.

Typical of Yellow Hair's vengeful spirit is the story related by William Warren in his *History of the Ojibway People*:

As we have mentioned, the Ojibwe and Sioux had entered into a truce so that they could hunt and trap in peace during a winter in the Crow Wing-Long Prairie Rivers area. To cement the truce, it had become the custom of individual warriors to adopt one another from different tribes as brothers. Yellow Hair and a Dakota Sioux warrior adopted each other and became friends. Yellow Hair, who already spoke some Sioux, perfected his mastery of the tongue. In the spring, just before their return to Leech Lake, four Ojibwe children, including Yellow Hair's eldest son, (Flat Mouth's brother) were murdered while at play by a marauding band of Sioux from the west.

Yellow Hair urged revenge. His followers and other Ojibwe chiefs felt this would be useless because the war party was long gone. Yellow Hair, however, argued for revenge against any available Sioux, including those with whom they had a peace treaty. Others urged moderation, and the chief finally agreed to return to Leech Lake with the bodies of the children. After burial, however, Yellow Hair and five of his warriors headed back for the Long Prairie intent upon revenge. They encountered the Sandy Lake band who were on their way home. The leadership of this group perceived Yellow Hair's purpose and tried to dissuade him, knowing that a resumption of hostilities would escalate making it impossible to hunt and trap in peace during future winters. They even gave him more than enough gifts to "cover" the death of his son.[1] Yellow Hair accepted the gifts and pretended to return to Leech Lake. However, when they were out of sight, he again turned southwest. William Warren[2] described the eventual gratification of Yellow Hair's loss thus:

On the head waters of Crow River, nearly two hundred miles from the point of his departure, Yellow Hair at last caught up with the two lodges of his enemies. At the first peep of dawn in the morning, the Dakotas were startled from their quiet slumbers by the fear-striking Ojibwe war-whoop, and as the men arose to grasp their arms, and the women and children jumped up in affright, the bullets of the enemy fell amongst them, causing wounds and death. After the first moments of surprise, the men of the Dakotas returned the fire of the enemy, and for many minutes the fight raged hotly. An interval in the incessant firing at last took place, and the voice of a Dakota, apparently wounded, called out to the Ojibways, "Alas! why is it that I die? I thought my road was clear before and behind me, and that the skies were cloudless above me. My mind dwelt only on good, and blood was not in my thoughts."

Yellow Hair recognized the voice of the warrior who had agreed to be his adopted brother during the late peace between their respective tribes. He understood his words, but his wrong was great, and his heart had become as hard as flint. He answered: "My brother, I too thought that the skies were cloudless above me, and I lived without fear; but a wolf came and destroyed my young; he tracked from the country of the Dakotas. My brother, for this you die!"

"My brother, I knew it not," answered the Dakota—"it was none of my people, but the wolves of the prairies."

The Ojibway warrior now quietly filled and lit his pipe, and while he smoked, the silence was only broken by the groans of the wounded, and the suppressed wail of bereaved mothers. Having finished his smoke, he laid aside his pipe, and once more he called out to the Dakotas:

"My brother, have you still in your lodge a child who will take the place of my lost one, whom your wolves have devoured? I have come a great distance to behold once more my young as I once beheld him, and I return not on my tracks till I am satisfied!"

The Dakotas, thinking that he wished for a captive to adopt instead of his deceased child, and happy to escape certain destruction at such a cheap sacrifice, took one of the surviving children, a little girl, and decking it with such finery and ornaments as they possessed, they sent her out to the covert of the Ojibway warrior. The innocent little girl came forward, but no sooner was she within reach of the avenger, than he grasped her by the hair of the head and loudly exclaiming—"I sent for thee that I might do with you as your people did to my child. I wish to behold thee as I once beheld him," he deliberately scalped her alive, and sent her shrieking back to her agonized parents.

After this cold-blooded act, the fight was renewed with great fury. Yellow Hair rushed desperately forward, and by main force he pulled down one of the Dakota lodges. As he did so the wounded warrior, his former adopted brother, discharged his gun at his breast, which the active and wary Ojibway adroitly dodged, the contents killed one of his comrades who had followed him close at his back. Not a being in that Dakota lodge survived; the other, being bravely defended, was left standing; and Yellow Hair, with his four surviving companions, returned homeward, their vengeance fully glutted, and having committed a deed which ever after became the topic of the lodge circles of their people.

Fortunately, Flat Mouth differed in many ways from his father. The practice of using poisons, for example, was abandoned once he succeeded him as a Pillager[3] chief.

Ukkewaus' War Party - Poorly Conceived, Poorly Executed

Uk-ke-waus was not really a chief but he led a reluctant band of forty-five Leech Lake warriors on a raid of Sioux villages in the Leaf Lakes and Battle Lake area. At the outset, the majority of Leech Lake Indians was anxious to organize a war party against the Sioux. Jean Baptiste Cadotte (son of the Cadotte who was one of the first men to have contact with the Ojibwe) had established a trading post at Cass Lake. When the Pillagers came to him for powder and shot, he persuaded them not to go on the warpath. However, when they returned to Leech Lake with some liquor, a wild celebration was held. The next morning, Uk-ke-waus dared the braves to follow him on a mission of revenge against the Dakota Sioux. Of the forty-five who answered his call, less than one-third returned. In a violent battle at Battle Lake (from which the lake received its name), Uk-ke-waus and all four of his sons were killed. He and his three oldest sons had fought to their deaths in a delaying action against a large number of Dakotas so that the handful of remaining Ojibwe might escape. It was said that the brave sacrifice was made because of the guilt Uk-ke-waus felt for his foolishness in organizing the war party.

This is another example of how far warriors would travel to wage war.

Dakotas Attack A French Trading Post
At The Mouth Of The Partridge

This tale is also from the lips of Chief Flat Mouth (the elder) of the Leech Lake Pillagers - and was told first hand to William Warren, the Ojibwe historian.

One winter, when Flat Mouth was a child and too young to bear arms (early 1780), he accompanied members of his tribe to the confluence of the Partridge (or Pena River) and the Crow Wing, where a French trader had constructed a post only that fall. The Ojibwe called the trader "Ah-wish-to-yah," which meant "Blacksmith." Several voyageurs were there with him at the time and together with the Pillager hunters and trappers totaled about forty men working out of the post. Most of the Indians had brought their families with them, even though they knew there was a good chance of an encounter with Dakota Sioux hunters or even war parties. The trader was also aware of the danger, but a heavy population of beaver had drawn him there.

Expecting the worst, the men erected a log barricade around the post and the wigwams.

Late one night, ten of the Pillager hunters awakened those at the post with the alarming news that a sizable band of Dakotas were in the area. They had crossed their trail and identified them by the lingering smell of tobacco (which was distinctly different from the ground inner-bark of the kinnikinnick smoked by the Ojibwe). The Dakota Sioux were following a trail which would lead them to a small, defenseless camp of Pillager hunters. Craftily, the Ojibwe circled ahead of the Sioux and crossed the trail, hoping to lure them to the more easily defended barricade at the trading post. The strategy worked. By the time the Dakota Sioux arrived, the barricade had been strengthened and nearly twenty men (French and Ojibwe) were ready for the attack.

The party of Dakota Sioux was large indeed - about two hundred braves - but whereas the men at the post were all armed with guns, the Dakota Sioux were forced to depend on bows and arrows and had only a half-dozen rifles among them.

The huge war party finally appeared on the bank across from the trading post. Confident in their numerical superiority, they leisurely put on their paint, feathers, and other ornaments. Then, sounding their war whoops, they charged across the ice sending out a cloud of arrows into the fortification. But the defenders were well-protected and their rifle fire was devastating. No Dakota Sioux warrior reached the barricade. With a change in strategy, the Sioux began firing their arrows almost straight up, lobbing them - like mortar fire - into the compound. The shower of barbed missiles was more effective and two Ojibwe hunters were wounded seriously enough to take them out of action. Some took refuge in the post itself. But in the end, the rifles proved to be more than an equalizing factor and a frustrated Dakota Sioux war party - with a greatly diminished supply of arrows - finally recognized the futility of the situation.

Before leaving, they cut holes in the river ice and gave their dead a watery burial[4].

Shortly after their departure, other hunters and trappers who had heard the shooting arrived at the post - about twenty reinforcements in all. Realizing that the Dakotas were nearly out of arrows, they wanted to press their advantage by pursuing them. The trader argued to the contrary and finally prevailed.

It is interesting that at this date, about 1780, the Dakotas had so few guns. It may have been that they came from the western prairies and had, therefore, little opportunity to procure them.

Two Examples of Late 18th Century Battles Between The Ojibwe And The Dakota Sioux[5]

Great Marten (Keche-wa-bi-she-shi), described as one of Bi-aus-wa's great war chiefs who led many raids from the Sandy Lake-Leech Lake area against the Dakota Sioux, perhaps deserves more credit than any other man for maintaining Ojibwe control of the Minnesota lake region.

The first campaign - under Great Marten's leadership - originated at Sandy Lake and included about 120 braves. It would be fair to speculate that some of the warriors might have come from the Leech-Cass Lake area, inasmuch as it was customary to invite participation from neighboring villages when large parties were organized. A runner was sometimes sent from village to village bearing something symbolic belonging to the leader, such as a pipe or tomahawk - along with an invitation to join the campaign.

By the time of this first incursion, the Mississippi had become the favorite warpath of the Ojibwe in their attempts to expand their frontiers to the south and make their lake region villages more safe from Sioux attack. As the war party proceeded down the river, Great Marten sent a canoe of scouts ahead and runners along each bank to make certain there would be no ambush. A short distance above the mouth of the Elk River, the scouts heard voices of the Dakota dialect. Quickly and silently they turned their canoe, moved in tight to the shoreline, and worked their way back upstream without detection. When they came into sight of their main party they threw water up in the air with their paddles to signify danger and that the war party should turn in to the eastern bank. After quickly applying war paint and adorning their hair with eagle feathers,[6] they ran in disorder through the wooded river bottoms until they came to the open prairie. Before them was a line of Dakota Sioux warriors in battle dress, apparently starting on the warpath against some northern Ojibwe destination. Great Marten's men, all "psyched-up" for battle, charged out onto the prairie. When the parties were in gun range of each other they opened fire. Because there was no cover, the only defense was to keep in motion. It must have been a spectacular sight - the painted and plumed bodies leaping continually from side to side - accented by war whoops and gun fire. Although the two bands were about equal in size, the late arriving Ojibwe kept pouring from the woods and the Dakotas, assuming they would soon be badly outnumbered, turned and fled, leaving behind their blankets and other paraphernalia they were carrying for their raid in the north. A running flight continued for about three miles, when the Dakota Sioux met a large party from another Dakota village, apparently on their way to join them in their campaign against the Ojibwe. Now the tide turned and Great Marten's braves took flight. Upon reaching a grove of oak trees they made a stand. The Dakota Sioux were without cover and dug holes in the ground (fox holes are not an innovation of our times) and so the battle continued. As the Dakotas tried to dig in closer they suffered numerous casualties. Then, noting a stiff south wind and the dry prairie grass killed during the recent winter, the Dakota Sioux set a fire. The Ojibwe were soon routed from the oak grove and lost three of their number to the encircling flames. The prairie fire did, however, give them time to flee to the river and take refuge on an island. Although the battle continued for some time, an impasse was reached and the war-weary Indians finally returned to their respective villages. The Ojibwe claimed the Dakotas had suffered severe losses but admitted to losing eight warriors in addition to the three lost in the fire. Since the Ojibwe of that day were recognized as superior marksmen (they may have been using guns for more years than the Sioux) it is entirely possible that the report is fairly accurate.

The following year, Great Marten led a second campaign down the Mississippi. This time the war party was smaller in number - about sixty braves. At exactly the same spot where the Ojibwe had fought the Dakota Sioux the previous year, they again encountered a war party. But this time the invaders were seriously outnumbered - estimates ran as high as 400 Dakotas. Overnight, Great Marten's warriors dug in, taking time to dig fox holes up to three feet deep which would hold up to two men. The Dakota Sioux, meanwhile, had taken possession of a wooded area in range of the Ojibwe. Even though the Sioux completely outnumbered the Ojibwe, they were in no hurry to sacrifice their men with an open charge. Occasionally, a more daring brave would make a move and pay for it with his life. Then an equally brave (or foolish) enemy would dash out from cover to secure the scalp. Others would try to retrieve the body to prevent mutilation (which many believed could adversely effect the fallen brave's after-life). Hand to hand skirmishes resulted. On one such foray Great Marten - who had tempted death on scores of occasions over the years - lost his life. The Dakota Sioux had also suffered losses and that night retreated some distance. The Ojibwe, discouraged and saddened by the loss of their leader, returned to their canoes under the shelter of darkness and headed for the north country.

The point of land between the Elk and Mississippi Rivers - where both battles were fought - was thereafter called "Me-gaud-e-win-ing" or "Battle Ground."

It is difficult to comprehend the dangers and uncertainties of living in the continent's heartland during this hundred year period. Not only was there open warfare with muskets - not just bows and arrows - but no village, no hunter, not even the women and children gathering wild rice or maple sap were safe from the marauding bands of Ojibwe and Dakota Sioux warriors.

The Cross Lake Massacre

Early in the spring of 1800 (or thereabouts) Ojibwe villagers from Sandy Lake and Mille Lacs Lake were returning from their winter hunt and were encamped on what is now called Battle Point on Cross Lake - north of present day Brainerd. It is likely the winter hunting camp was where the prairie meets the pines west of there.

Legend has it that the advance guard of the Dakota Sioux approached on the ice "on all fours" disguised with wolf hides.

According to Ojibwe tradition, the Dakota Sioux war party contained about 400 warriors while the Ojibwe had only half that number including women and children. The encampment was nearly annihilated. She-shebe, an Ojibwe warrior, was one of the handful who escaped and for his heroic actions became a hero to his tribe.

Some Of Flat Mouth's Raids On The Dakota Sioux

Although Flat Mouth was usually a man of peace, he not only defended the area against Dakota Sioux attacks, but participated in raiding parties to the west and south, almost always organized for reasons of revenge. These raids were often in alliance with tribes from other lakes. A frequent ally was Ba-be-sig-undi-bay or "Curly Head", the principal chief of the Gull Lake and Crow Wing Ojibwe. On one occasion, the two chiefs joined forces to avenge the deaths of Flat Mouth's nephew and two of Curly Head's allies: Waubo-o-jeeg (name-sake of the famous Wisconsin chief of the previous century) and She-shebe (hero of the Cross Lake massacre).[7] Their joint forces nearly wiped out a Dakota Sioux village

Courtesy of the Cass County Historical Society.

Eshke-bog-e-coshe (Flat-Mouth) of Leech Lake. Bust by Francis Vincenti. Location: Senate wing, third floor, east. (One of only three Indian statues in the U.S. Capitol).

in the Long Prairie area. A handful of Sioux prevented the Ojibwe from taking scalps, but Flat Mouth and Curly Head returned to their respective lakes with their desire for revenge satisfied. The Dakota Sioux never again attempted to establish a permanent village in the Long Prairie area.

In the spring of 1832, Flat Mouth led a party against the Dakota Sioux west of the Crow Wing River, possibly in the Wadena area. Three Sioux were killed and another three wounded. He lost one of his own men: an ally from Cass Lake.

We told earlier how Uk-ke-waus of Leech Lake led an unsuccessful raiding party against the Dakota Sioux at Battle Lake. Only the sacrifice of his own life and the lives of his three sons, as they fought a delaying action, permitted the others to escape. A young Flat Mouth joined about 130 Red Lake warriors (some of them relatives of Uk-ke-waus) in avenging their deaths. He was on his way home from visiting his Cree relatives in the north and had stopped to hunt with friends at Red Lake. He later recalled that it was winter and they used snow shoes until they reached the windswept prairies to the west. He also told of impressive herds of buffalo along the way. Although it was preferred to take revenge against those who had killed your own people, satisfaction was often achieved by retaliating against whomever was available from that tribe. This was apparently the case here. The avengers came upon a Dakota Sioux village of about 50 lodges and fired volley after volley into the teepees. Heavy fire was returned and the small Ojibwe army retreated—satisfied that appropriate retaliation had been taken. Flat Mouth and two other warriors stayed behind, however, and approached the village once again under cover of darkness. They emptied their guns into a group of mourners and then escaped into the night.

Flat Mouth also told William Warren of his conquest of the Yankton-Sioux chief, Shappa. The story begins with Flat Mouth and his family camped on Otter Tail Lake at the outlet of Otter Tail Creek. Other members of the Leech Lake band were scattered throughout the area—hunting, trapping, and collecting wild rice. A huge Yankton Sioux war party (400 by Flat Mouth's estimates) passed through the area, moving in the direction of Battle Lake. Fortunately, they missed all Ojibwe camps except an outpost on a small unnamed lake where two of Flat Mouth's cousins were taking beaver. The two Pillagers fought bravely, killing three Sioux and wounding others. They were successful in retreating to a small rock outcropping on the lake, but were still in range of both guns and arrows from the shore. They quickly erected a rock wall. The Yankton Sioux, however, cut logs which they floated and pushed in front of them as they approached the islet. The Pillagers finally ran out of ammunition and it was all over.

In examining the campsite the Yankton Sioux had used the night before, Flat Mouth found that four Yankton Chiefs had left their identification marks on trees, including the beaver image of Chief Shappa. After returning to Leech Lake, Flat Mouth sent his warpipe and warclub to neighboring villages, seeking to recruit an army of vengeance. Meanwhile, Shappa heard of the Ojibwe plans, probably through Col. Dickson[8] who was married to his sister, and sent word to Flat Mouth through the Englishman that he had not been involved in the murder of his cousins and wanted to talk peace. He asked that there be a meeting at a trading post located on the Red River. Flat Mouth chose 30 of his best braves and set out for the powwow. When he arrived at the trading post, he found four Frenchmen in charge. The next day Shappa arrived with only two of his braves. Flat Mouth made it clear from the outset that he did not believe the Sioux Chief's claim of innocence and refused to smoke the peace pipe. Shappa knew he was doomed and spent the night praying and singing to the spirits. For some reason, Flat Mouth did not want to witness the bloodshed, so he asked his men to take the three Yankton Sioux out on the prairies, away from the Trading Post—so as not to involve the white men— and do what they wished with the captives. Flat Mouth did tell his men, however, that he would take responsibility for their deeds. The men did as told and after shooting the braves, cut off their heads.

Col. Dickson was naturally very upset by the death of his brother-in-law and told Flat Mouth that the trading posts on Leech Lake would be closed. It proved to be an idle threat, but was one more factor in the escalating enmity between the red-bearded trader and Chief Flat Mouth.

It is interesting that we have no record of Flat Mouth ever initiating any action against the Sioux; his acts of aggression were taken in retaliation.

White Efforts to Establish Peace

Lieutenant Zebulon Pike

In 1805, Pike journeyed up the Mississippi in search of the source of the river. He was formally commissioned by General James Wilkinson (sometimes suspected of treasonous intent because of his friendship with Aaron Burr) to explore and take possession of the country (which had become a part of the United States through the Louisiana Purchase of 1803) and to gain permission from the Indians to construct a military fort and trading houses at strategic locations. Pike's subsequent negotiations with the Dakota Sioux were particularly significant in Minnesota history because Fort Snelling was later constructed on property secured as a result of the agreement reached with the Sioux.

Another purpose of his mission was to bring peace between the warring Dakota Sioux and Ojibwe and to advise both that they were now under American jurisdiction.

On February 16, 1906, Pike held a council with the chiefs of the Mississippi headwaters area. In his opening speech he said,

"I was chosen to ascend the Mississippi to bear to his red children the words of their father, and the Great Spirit has opened the eyes

and ears of all the nations to listen to my words. The Sauks and Reynards are planting corn and raising cattle. The Winnebagos continue peaceable as usual, and even the Sioux have laid by the hatchet at my request. Yes, my brothers, the Sioux who have so long and obstinately warred against the Chippewas, have agreed to lay by the hatchet, smoke the calumet, and again become your brothers. Brothers! You behold the pipe of Wabasha as a proof of what I say. The Little Corbeau, Fils de Pinchon, and L'Aile Roughe, had marched two hundred and fifty warriors to revenge the blood of their women and children, slain last year at the St. Peters. I sent a runner after them, stopped their march, and met them in council at the mouth of the St. Peters, where they promised to remain peaceable until my return; and if the Ouchipawah[9] chiefs accompanied me, to receive them as brothers, and accompany us to St. Louis, there to bury the hatchet, and smoke the pipe in the presence of our great war-chief; and to request him to punish those who first broke the peace...Brothers! I understand that one of your young men killed an American at Red Lake last year, but that the murderer is far off; let him keep so; send him where we may never hear of him more, for were he here I would be obliged to demand him of you, and make my young men shoot him."

A Red Lake Indian, Chief "Old Sweet" was present, and responded thus,

"My father! I have heard and understood the words of our great father. It overjoys me to see you make peace among us. I should have accompanied you had my family been present, and would have gone to see their father, the great war-chief.

"The medal I hold in my hand I received from the English chiefs. I willingly deliver it up to you. Wabasha's calumet with which I am presented, I receive with all my heart. Be assured that I will use my best endeavors to keep my young men quiet. There is my calumet, I send it to my father the great war-chief. What does it signify that I should go to see him?

"My father! you will meet the Sioux on your return. You may make them smoke in my pipe, and tell them that I have let fall my hatchet.

"My father! tell the Sioux on the upper part of the St. Peters River, that they mark trees with the figure of a calumet, that we of Red Lake who go that way, should we see them, may make peace with them, being assured of their pacific disposition, when we shall see the calumet marked on the trees."

Courtesy of the Cass County Historical Society.

Views at Fort Snelling, Minnesota. The site was negotiated during the conclave between Zebulon Pike and the Dakota Sioux.

Flat Mouth gave similar assurances and designated his brother, Beau, and another chief called "The Buck" as personal emissaries to travel with Pike to visit the Dakota Sioux and then go on to St. Louis.

Pike's efforts and the efforts of others culminated in a peace treaty between the southern Ojibwe and the Dakota Sioux at Prairie Du Chien (Wisconsin) in 1825 and at Fond du Lac the following year for the northern Ojibwe and the Dakota Sioux. The treaties did not make a great deal of difference and the fighting continued - as we shall see in the description which follows of Schoolcraft's meeting with Flat Mouth.

Henry Schoolcraft - 1832

Schoolcraft had been chosen by Governor Lewis Cass (of the Michigan Territory) as a member of his 1820 expedition up the Mississippi. At that time, Schoolcraft was known as an author and mineralogist. The 1820's Expedition apparently terminated at a lake Pike had called "Upper Red Cedar"; Schoolcraft renamed it "Cassina" in honor of the Governor. Today we call it "Cass Lake," and the lower lake we have named "Pike Bay".[10]

In 1832, Schoolcraft was an Indian Agent, and he organized his own expedition. As we know, he successfully identified Lake Itasca as the true source of the Mississippi River. Late on July 16th, accompanied by an escort of soldiers (under the command of Lt. James Allen) and Rev. William T. Boutwell (a Presbyterian missionary who was then stationed at Mackinac) Schoolcraft arrived at Leech Lake. Rev. Boutwell gives us a remarkable picture of an aging Flat Mouth in his report of the event in the Boston "Missionary Herald" in 1834:

The principal chief (Flat Mouth) sent his "Mishinne," waiting-man, requesting Mr. Schoolcraft to come and breakfast with him.

"Decorum required him to comply with the request, though he was at liberty to furnish the table mostly himself. A mat spread in the middle of the floor served as a table, upon which the dishes were placed. Around this were spread others upon which the guests sat while the wife of the chief waited upon the table, and poured the tea. She afterward took breakfast by herself.

After breakfast they proceeded to the chief's headquarters which was thus described:

"It is a building perhaps twenty feet by twenty-five, made of logs,

which I am informed was presented to him by one of the traders. As we entered, the old chief, bare-legged and bare-foot, sat with much dignity upon a cassette. A blanket, and cloth about the loins, covered his otherwise naked body, which was painted black. His chief men occupied a bench by his side, while forty or more of his warriors sat on the floor around the walls of his room smoking. The old man arose and gave us his hand as we were introduced, bidding us to take a seat at his right, on his bed. As I cast my eye around upon his savage group, for once, I wished I possessed the painter's skill. The old chief had again returned to his seat upon the large wooden trunk, and as if to sit a little more like a white man than an Indian, had thrown one leg across the other knee. His warriors were all feathered, painted, and equipped for service. Many of them wore the insignia of courage, a strip of polecat[11] skin around the head or heels, the bushy tail of the latter so attached as to drag on the ground; the crown of the head was ornamented with feathers, indicating the number of enemies the individual had killed, on one of which I counted no less than twelve.

"One side of his room was hung with an English and American flag, medals, war-clubs, lances, tomahawks, arrows, and other implements of death. The subject of vaccination was now presented to the chief, with which he was pleased, and ordered his people to assemble for that purpose. I stood by the doctor, and kept the minutes while he performed the business.

"Preparations were now made for taking our leave when the chief arose, and giving his hand to each, spoke as follows, in reply to Mr. Schoolcraft, who had addressed them as 'My children.' 'You call us children. We are not children, but men. When I think of the condition of my people I can hardly refrain from tears. It is so melancholy that even the trees weep over it. When I heard that you were coming to visit us, I felt inclined to go and meet you. I hoped that you would bring us relief. But if you did not furnish some relief, I thought I should go farther, to the people who wear big hats, in hopes of obtaining that relief from them, which the Long Knives (Americans) have so often promised.

Our great Father promised us, when we smoked the pipe with the Sioux at Prairie du Chien in 1825, and at Fond du Lac in 1826, that the first party who crossed the line, and broke the treaty, should be punished. This promise has not been fulfilled. Not a year has passed but some of our young men, our wives, and our children have fallen, and the blood that has begun to flow will not soon stop. I do not expect this year will close before more of my young men will fall. When my son was killed, about a year since, I determined not to lay down any arms as long as I can see the light of the sun. I do not think the Great Spirit ever made us to sit still and see our young men, our wives, and our children murdered.

"Since we have listened to the Long Knives, we have not prospered. They are not willing we should go ourselves, and flog our enemies, nor do they fulfill their promise and do it for us."

"The medals of each chief and a string of wampum were now brought forth stained with vermilion.

"See our medals," and holding them up by the strings, he continued: "These and all your letters are stained with blood. I return them all to you to make them bright. None of us wish to receive them back," laying them at Mr. Schoolcraft's feet, "until you have wiped off the blood."

"Here a shout of approbation was raised by all his warriors present, and the old man, growing more eloquent, forgot that he was holding his blanket around his naked body with one hand, and it dropped from about him, and he proceeded: "The words of the Long Knives have passed through our forests as a rushing wind, but they have been words merely. They have only shaken the trees, but have not stopped to break them down, nor even to make the rough places smooth."

"It is not that we wish to be at war with the Sioux, but when they enter our country and kill our people, we are obliged to revenge their death. Nor will I conceal from you the fact that I have already sent tobacco and pipestems to different bands to invite them to come to our relief. We have been successful in the late war, but we do not feel that we have taken sufficient revenge."

"Here a bundle of sticks two inches long was presented, indicating the number of Ojibwe killed by the Sioux since the treaty of 1825, amounting to forty-three.[12] Just as we were ready to embark, the old man came out in his regimentals, a military coat faced with red, ruffled shirt, hat, pantaloons, gloves, and shoes. So entirely changed was his appearance that I did not recognize him until he spoke."

Hole-in-the-Day I

Curly Head, the legendary Gull Lake Chief, in his last years was served by two protege's - brothers - whom he named as his "pipe bearers:" the older of the brothers (by two years) was Song-a-cumig or "Firm Ground," and the other was to become the famous Pugona-geshig or Hole-in-the-Day I.

The brothers had come to Minnesota with the Cass Expedition in 1820, for which they were awarded medals by this famous governor of the Michigan Territory. Although younger than Firm Ground, Hole-in-the-Day was the more dynamic and out-going. Before the 1820's were over, he had been named a sub-chief at Sandy Lake; shortly after the death of Curly Head, he moved his young family to Gull Lake and soon took over as the principal chief of the Indians of that lake and the Crow Wing River. He is believed to have had his headquarters on the thoroughfare between Gull and Round Lakes. Hole-in-the-Day gathered his rice in the small lake nearby which now bears his name and collected sap from the maple trees in the wooded area between Round Lake and Long Lake - now Ojibwe Park.

Historian Carl Zapffe in his book, "The Man Who Lived in Three Centuries," gives an enlightening account of collaboration between the hero of his work, John Smith, and Chief Hole-in-the-Day. It seems Hole-in-the-Day's medicine man had a vision of a Dakota Sioux village which could be easily conquered and said that he could lead his chief to its location. Hole-in-the-Day asked John Smith if he cared to join him. Zapffe gives this account of Smith's response and the expedition that followed:

"Not forgetting my early pledge to spill the blood of those who had murdered my sister and brother," later recorded Smith, "I consented gladly; and, summoning all the warriors of my then great tribe, we started out upon the warpath." The combined assault was headed by Hole-in-the-Day, though guided by the Medicine Man. Three days passed in transit; and on the morning of the fourth the stage of the stealthy approach began.

Sure enough! Exactly in the position predicted by the Medicine Man, there stood a Dakota village, lying peaceably in a small valley. From one of the lodges issued a thin and lazy column of smoke. Otherwise there was no noise, neither any signs of life.

Creeping with exceeding precaution, the warriors came within gunshot, and the Chief gave the fatal signal. A simultaneous volley thundered down the little valley, lead balls pouring with well-considered spacing into every one of the teepees. The only answer was the dismal howl of a dog.

Because Smith's sole purpose in agreeing to accompany Hole-in-the-Day was to discover an opportunity for revenging the deaths in his family, he now boldly stepped forward to take the initiative in bringing this battle to its hoped-for climax.

Furthermore, deep inside he felt extremely confident "that no enemy bullet could kill me, as I hold a charmed life."

Not waiting to reload his gun, and grabbing nothing but his battleaxe, Smith raced to the nearest lodge — the one having a slight issue of smoke. He bounded right through the doorway, and with such fierce energy as calculated to take any opponent by surprise. But he found nothing except the dog. The exciting wisps of smoke were issuing from a few lazy embers, apparently remaining from a fire that had been abandoned hours before. Plunging his tomahawk into the body of the unfortunate dog, Smith dashed back outside and ordered his warriors to search the village. All dwellings proved to be empty.

Hole-in-the-Day was so intensely angered over this useless enterprise that he immediately killed "Big Medicine Man."

After spending a few years at Gull Lake, Hole-in-the-Day moved south to the mouth of the Crow Wing and, later, to the mouth of the Little Elk River, just north of the site of present-day Little Falls. Here he protected the southern frontier of the Ojibwe. At times the pressures from the Dakota Sioux were too much and he would be forced to retreat to Whitefish or Rabbit Lake. So far as we know, he never did return to Gull Lake to live.

In 1838, Hole-in-the-Day played a major role in a series of bloody confrontations between the Dakotas and the Ojibwe. In April of that year, he and a party of nine braves stumbled onto a camp of Sioux on the Chippewa River (a tributary of the Minnesota); they were mostly women and children temporarily separated from a hunting party. Professing peace, they were warmly welcomed and dined on dog meat - one of the Indians' choice delicacies. That night, on signal, Hole-in-the-Day and his men fell on the Dakota Sioux and killed all but three.

On August 2, Sioux relatives of the massacre victims had an opportunity for revenge. They surprised Hole-in-the-Day and five companions near Fort Snelling; one of the Indians with whom Hole-in-the-Day had exchanged clothing - or ornaments - was killed and another wounded (both were Ottawas). When one of the Dakota Sioux ran in to collect what he believed to be the scalp of Hole-in-the-Day, White Fisher, who was in the Ojibwe party, shot him. The famous Indian Agent, Taliaferro, came on the scene at that point, and the Sioux fled. The Ojibwe were taken to the fort and the Ottawa Indian was buried there. Hole-in-the-Day was escorted across the river and had to find his way home on his own.

When they heard of the incident, the chiefs of the neighboring Dakota Sioux villages came to the fort, as well as the leadership of the Red Wing band of Lake Pepin - to which the young Sioux belonged who had killed the Ottawa.

At the insistence of the commander of the fort, Major Plympton, two young braves were turned over to him and placed in custody, but the chiefs pleaded for their lives. After being satisfied that the Dakota Sioux leadership would properly punish their young warriors, Major Plympton released them to their custody. The punishment administered by the ranking Sioux braves to the culprits was traditional: their blankets, leggings and breech cloths were cut into small pieces; their hair was cut short (signifying great humiliation); and they were heavily flogged. One Ojibwe was dead; one Dakota Sioux was dead; the score was even, and it seemed peace would be continued.

However, the following year, 1839, Hole-in-the-Day with five hundred of his own people, another hundred from the Crow Wing area, one hundred fifty from Leech Lake, and another contingent from Mille Lacs Lake all arrived at the St. Peter's Agency (by the fort) under the mistaken notion that they could collect the treaty payments due them. Twelve hundred Dakota Sioux arrived at the agency for the same purpose (but under a different treaty). The Ojibwe were told they would have to go to La Pointe to collect what they had coming, but they were given some food. Surprisingly enough, the historic enemies got along well and even danced and played games together. After a month, the Ojibwe began their return journeys to the north. Two of Hole-in-the-Day's men who were related to the warrior shot the previous year stopped at the fort to weep over the grave of their slain kinsman. Inspired to seek revenge, they approached the Lake Calhoun camp of the Dakotas at night—some think with the knowledge and encouragement of Hole-in-the-Day. At daybreak they killed a departing hunter named Nika. The slain Sioux turned out to be a highly respected warrior, brother-in-law of the chief, and nephew of the famous medicine man, Red Bird.

Revenge came quickly. One contingent of about one hundred warriors - under Little Crow (a predecessor of the Little Crow who led the Sioux uprising in 1862) - surprised a large bank of Ojibwe near the present site of Stillwater. They were finally driven off but not before killing twenty-one and wounding twenty-nine Ojibwe. The second contingent, under Red Bird, pursued the Mille Lacs Lake band. Before leaving, the pipe of war was passed down the rows of Dakota Sioux warriors and Red Bird followed, laying hands on the heads of each and swearing them to strike without pity, taking no captives. After locating the Mille Lacs Indians, they waited until most braves had gone on ahead to hunt. The old men, women, and children left behind were at first easy prey, but the hunters returned quickly and a bitter struggle ensued. The Dakota Sioux took seventy scalps but lost seventeen braves of their own, including Red Bird and his son. The Ojibwe scalps were hung from their lodge poles at Lake Calhoun and the celebrating went on for a month.

Taliaferro, the Indian agent, was keenly disappointed and left the agency soon thereafter. He had taken a special interest and pride in the Lake Calhoun settlement where he had been quite successful in encouraging agricultural practices. He had given the settlement the name "Eatonville." And so the bloody conflict between the two great tribes continued for another generation.[13]

Chief Hole-in-the-Day died in 1847 at an age of about forty-six years. He was returning from Pigs Eye (St. Paul) where he had consumed so much alcohol he was being carried home on the floor of a wagon. As the entourage was crossing the Platte River he fell from the wagon and was critically injured. His warriors carried him to a nearby home; here he regained consciousness long enough to pass on the mantle of authority and a few words of wisdom to his son - Kwi-wi-sens (or "Boy"). When he died, he was buried according to his instructions on Baldur Bluff - overlooking the Mississippi. Here, in death, it is said he continues his vigil for the canoes of the Dakota Sioux.

Chief Hole-in-the-Day II

By 1855, Hole-in-the-Day II, son of Hole-in-the-Day the elder, was recognized by the whites as the principal chief of the Gull Lake-Crow Wing Ojibwe - and was so designated in the treaty signed that year establishing the Gull Lake Reservation. This action was not well received by all Ojibwe. Some of the Gull Lake leadership was especially unhappy and Kwi-wi-sens-ish, or "Bad Boy", was sufficiently disgruntled to leave Gull Lake a couple of years later and take up residence at Mille Lacs Lake.

Hole-in-the-Day got the attention of Territorial Governor Ramsey and most Minnesotans in 1850 when he and a small party (perhaps only one or two others) attacked six Dakota Sioux (taking one scalp) just across the river from St. Paul (after hiding in the gorge of Fountain Cave). The attack was probably in reprisal for the Dakota Sioux annihilation of a party of fifteen Ojibwe a little more than a month earlier on the Apple River in Wisconsin. Governor Ramsey summoned the chiefs of both the Dakota Sioux and the Ojibwe to a peace council at Fort Snelling. On June 9th, Hole-in-the-Day arrived with about 100 braves; late the following morning about 300 Sioux arrived on horseback; they dismounted in a display of pageantry and saluted the Ojibwe who had lined up to welcome them. Governor Ramsey presided personally at the council. William Warren, the Ojibwe historian whom we have quoted so liberally, read the charges against the Dakota Sioux, and Bad Hail read the counter-charges against the Ojibwe. All sides finally agreed to abide by the provisions of the treaty of 1843 and the council concluded with a feast.

Earlier in the proceedings the Dakota Sioux Chiefs had left the council in protest of the presence of some white women who were on hand as members of the Governor's party. Hole-in-the-Day scored a coup by offering the women seats among his people. However, the women thought it best to leave, and when the Dakotas returned they were sharply taken to task by Governor Ramsey. Though the council concluded peacefully and to the satisfaction of the Governor, mistrust on both sides was still evident as hostages were required to insure safe journeys home.

These were among the last of the confrontations between the Ojibwe and the Dakota Sioux, finally laying to rest more than 100 years of conflict. When it was over, the territories occupied by the two tribes were very much as they had been in 1766, when the Ojibwe had driven the Dakota Sioux from the woodlands and established their own villages. All of the fighting, all of the bloodshed, all of the heartache, all of the suffering had been for nothing!

[1] There were three ways in which an Ojibwe could receive satisfaction for the death of a loved one: (1) kill an enemy, (2) adopt one of the enemy—usually a child, or (3) be paid off in gifts.

[2] Warren, William, *History of the Ojibway People*, M.H.S.

[3] Ojibwe of Leech Lake. For more about the Pillagers, see *Tales of Four Lakes* by this author.

[4] It is surmised that one of the reasons for the watery burial was to prevent scalping.

[5] Warren, William, *History of the Ojibway*, Vol. 5, Minnesota Historical Collection.

[6] Each eagle plume represented a slain enemy or a scalp taken in battle.

[7] They and their families had been fishing through the ice on Mille Lacs Lake.

[8] Dickson was an English trader on Leech Lake at the time. He is also mentioned in Chapter VII.

[9] Chippewa (or Ojibwe).

[10] For Zebulon Pike.

[11] Skunk.

[12] Further indication of the continuation of the 100 Years War.

[13] Warren, William, *History of the Ojibway*, Minnesota Historical Collection, Vol. 5.

CHAPTER VII

CONFLICTS BETWEEN WHITES AND NATIVE AMERICANS

In contrast to the conflicts among the various Native American tribes, the conflicts between the Indians and the whites were relatively few in number in the North American heartland. Although explorers, missionaries, voyageurs, traders and early settlers may have had many anxious moments, there were relatively few actual hostilities. Unfortunately, some of these incidents resulted in many casualties. It is ironic that the most serious fighting — with by far the largest numbers of casualties on both sides — was among the last; it occurred in 1862 during the Civil War. In contrast, relationships during the first two centuries of contacts between the Native Americans and the whites in this part of the continent were friendly and peaceful.

Radisson tells how he was captured at the age of 16 by the Iroquois and would have been burned at the stake had it not been for the pleas of an Iroquois woman — but that was not in the Midwest or in central Canada. The French in particular feared the Iroquois and tried to avoid them as much as possible. This was the principal reason the French explorers and traders skipped over the eastern Great Lakes and concentrated on Lake Superior and points west. In contrast, early French explorers tell repeatedly of good relationships with the Native Americans in the North American heartland.

The first recorded killing of whites in the area described in this book (Minnesota and nearby Dakotas, Wisconsin, Ontario and Manitoba) was the Lake of the Woods massacre in 1736. Of course, the deaths of La Verendrye's eldest son, his priest and nineteen soldier-voyageurs was of major significance and, as we have seen, was used by the Cree, Monsonis and Assiniboin as an excuse to attack the Dakota Sioux of the Woodlands, even though it was their prairie cousins who had done the killing.

Zebulon Pike recorded that in 1804, the year before his exploration up the Mississippi, three Frenchmen had been mistaken for Dakota Sioux and killed by the Ojibwe.

Along with accidents and isolated incidents there were a few very serious conflicts, and we shall describe them in the balance of this chapter.

The Seven Oaks Massacre - 1816

Lord Selkirk, a Scotsman, had purchased the Hudson's Bay Company. In the early 1800s that company's chief rival for the fur trade was the North West Company[1] — organized by Montreal merchants. Selkirk had a great vision for the area granted to his company under charter from the King of England and he established a small colony of white settlers at Pembina. He called his new nation "Assiniboia".

The North West Company was very upset by this maneuver and organized an Indian raid on the colony. All twenty-two settlers, including the governor, Robert Semple, were slain and scalped.

One of the Indian raiders was Chief Maji-gobo, who eventually settled on Leech Lake and became an ally of Flat Mouth. Schoolcraft met Maji-gobo and described him as "tall, gaunt and savage looking". The chief was unashamed of his involvement in the massacre and took credit for personally murdering Governor Semple.

That was the end of the colony for a time, but later a large number of mostly Swiss settlers were brought in. In retaliation for the massacre, Selkirk's men captured all of the Northwest forts, including Fort William and Fort St. Louis (Duluth-Superior) on Lake Superior. The two companies were finally merged in 1821.

The War of 1812

Although several Canadian Ojibwe tribes aligned themselves with the British in the War of 1812, virtually none of the

Minnesota Ojibwe joined the English. However, every effort was made by the British to recruit the Minnesota Indians. Col. Robert Dickson,[2] who had made a career of trading with both the Dakotas and the Ojibwe, was perhaps the best known of the British agents who tried to persuade the Indians to fight against the Americans. He sent an interpreter by the name of St. Germain to Leech Lake to deliver presents and wampum belts to Flat Mouth as the most influential chief. A public meeting was held and Flat Mouth said (in later years to William Warren) that he had responded thus, "When I go to war against my enemies, I do not call on the whites to join my warriors. The white people have quarreled among themselves, and I do not wish to meddle in their quarrels, nor do I intend ever, even to be guilty of breaking the windowglass of a white man's dwelling."

Wabasha, a hereditary Dakota Sioux chief joined forces with Dickson; so did Joseph Renville — a Sioux half-breed and noted guide and interpreter who had served with Pike. Dickson and his Indian allies captured Mackinac without a shot, also Fort Shelby at Prairie du Chien.

British-Indian forces also quickly occupied the trading posts at Grand Portage and Fort St. Louis (Duluth-Superior).

Some historians believe that because the Ojibwe refused to join the British forces most of the Dakota Sioux felt they had to stay home to protect their villages from the Ojibwe. Had both tribes joined the English there could have been a serious second front against the seaboard states.

The Conflict of 1862

Southern Minnesota became the setting for the most devastating massacre of white settlers and resulting military reprisal against the Indian peoples in the nation's history. These atrocities, plus the annihilation of Custer and his men at Little Big Horn and the culmination of white man's further reprisals at Wounded Knee, taken together, are the most deplorable chapter in the history of white-Indian relations.

As with all wars, there were direct causes or incidents which triggered the fighting; but there were more significant indirect causes. Let us examine the latter first. The Sioux had many reasons for dissatisfaction and concern: (1) there was an obvious westward movement of whites and a ravenous hunger for land[3];

Courtesy of the Minnesota Historical Society.

Artist's rendition of The Attack on Fort Ridgely.

(2) Indian policies of the United States government were disheartening—treaty payments were late and meager, Indian Agents were political appointees, often ill prepared for their jobs, and the Indians were literally compressed into reservations; and (3) the very nature of the Sioux people, at least at that time, was aggressive and they were not accustomed to being pushed around without fighting back.

The incident that triggered this war was the killing of five whites by four Wahpeton Sioux braves on the farm of Howard Baker near Acton. Understanding the significance of the murders, the Sioux debated long into the night what course of action to take. Tradition holds that Little Crow opposed further violence against the whites, comparing the white soldiers who would come for revenge to "clouds of locust". It has been said that Little Crow yielded to his hot-blooded braves in fear that they would turn elsewhere for leadership. They had already turned not long before to another called Traveling Hail[4] for "chief speaker". And so the die was cast and the balance of the night was spent in preparation for attack. The next day, August 18, 1862, Little Crow led about two hundred warriors against the Redwood Indian Agency. Victory came easily.

There is evidence that the whites of Minnesota were completely surprised by the uprising. Frontier newspapers of the day gave no indication of immediate concern, even though it was common knowledge that the treaty payments due the Dakotas were long overdue.

In that summer of 1862, Captain John Marsh was in command of Fort Ridgely. In early August, Lt. Sheehan and his troops arrived. They had originally been stationed at Fort Ripley, but had been temporarily assigned to the Sioux Agency on the Yellow Medicine River (for about six weeks). On August 17, Sheehan and his men were ordered to return to Fort Ripley, thus leaving about 85 men at Ridgely under Marsh's command.

August 18, one day after Sheehan's forces left for Fort Ripley, was the day the conflict began. When Captain Marsh learned of trouble at the Lower Agency (12 miles above the Fort) he sent a messenger to catch Sheehan and bring him back. Meanwhile, Marsh set out with 46 men for the Sioux Agency. When only a few miles out of the fort, he found farm homes in flames and the bodies of numerous settlers. Upon reaching the Redwood ferry, across from the agency, he found the boatman dead and the ferry across the river. A well-known Sioux, White Dog, appeared and assured the captain it was safe to cross.

When Marsh had committed his men to the crossing, White Dog fired his gun and dove for cover. Scores of Indians were in hiding and opened fire. After a lengthy and bloody battle in which many were killed on both sides, including Captain Marsh who drowned, the surviving troops retreated to the fort, leaving behind twenty-six dead soldiers.

Lt. Sheehan and his men, having received Marsh's message, returned to Fort Ridgley. This brought the total number of soldiers at the fort to 180. About 300 settlers and members of military families were also at the fort, seeking protection. The Sioux attacked the fort on the 20th. An eight-day siege followed. It was estimated that Little Crow's forces numbered 1,500. But the fort held. More than 100 Indians were killed, while the military lost only six because of the fortifications.

On August 28, Col. Sibley arrived with an army of 1600 men; the Sioux withdrew. It was now only a matter of time until Little Crow's forces would be driven from the state. But the Sioux scored many victories in the early fighting, including (1) the victory over Captain Marsh's troops at the Lower Agency, (2) more than fifty members of German farm families in Brown and Nicollet counties killed on the first day of fighting, and (3) at Birch Coulee, where more than eighty soldiers were killed.

Little Crow attacked New Ulm twice, but the community survived behind temporary fortifications.

Estimates ran to more than five hundred whites killed and thousands wounded; the number of Indian casualties remains unknown but could have been even higher. In a matter of weeks it was all over. Sheer numbers made the difference. The Battle of Wood Lake was fought on September 23. Although a massive action, only seven soldiers were killed or died later as a result. There was a futile Sioux attack on Fort Abercombie[5] a few days later, followed by isolated skirmishes, but the war was over. Little Crow and his surviving warriors fled to the Dakotas and Canada. The Battle of the Little Big Horn and the tragedy of Wounded Knee were yet to come, along with dozens of smaller skirmishes, but for the North American Heartland there would be only one more armed clash between whites and Indians, and that would be at Leech Lake thirty-six years later.

As an aftermath to the war, more than 307 Sioux prisoners were condemned to death. Because of the huge number, Col. Sibley decided to share the burden of decision by referring the final judgment to General Pope. The general, in turn, passed it on to that desk "where the buck always stops"—President Lincoln, himself. Episcopal Bishop Henry Whipple urged the president to show mercy. Even though already heavily burdened by the great Civil War, President Lincoln ordered a review of each case individually and expressed his desire that no man should die merely because he participated in the war. Only those who had killed civilians or were guilty of rape (just two cases) were to pay with their lives. Finally, on Lincoln's written orders, thirty-eight Sioux warriors were hanged, simultaneously, in Mankato on December 26, 1862. It is surmised by some historians that Lincoln wanted to show mercy but believed a significant number had to hang to satisfy the whites of Minnesota. There is little evidence that justice was a major concern.

Once the conflict had subsided and the Sioux driven to the Dakotas and Canada, the regular military left Fort Ridgely and returned to Fort Snelling. The Minnesota Volunteers resumed responsibility for manning the fort. Following the Civil War, the regular military returned to Fort Ridgely and replaced the volunteers. They remained until May of 1867, when the fort was closed.

A bounty of 25¢ was offered for any Sioux scalp taken in Minnesota. Little Crow was killed while hunting deer[6] in the state. His body was dragged through the streets of New Ulm and thrown in the town dump. Later he was given a burial.

Ojibwe-White Conflict Narrowly Averted (also 1862)

As Little Crow was leading the Dakotas and other Sioux against the Redwood Agency, Hole-in-the-Day the younger was at the very same time directing the obliteration of the St. Columbia Mission by several hundred Ojibwe warriors who had been gathered from as far as Sandy Lake to the east and Ottertail on the west. Why did the wily chieftain choose the little church on the shores of Gull Lake as the subject of his first attack when he could have chosen strategic Fort Ripley or the white settlement of Crow Wing? First of all, the mission not only symbolized white man but it also represented his foreign religion. Secondly, Hole-in-the-Day may have been waiting for expected reinforcements from Leech Lake. If, in truth, there was collaboration between the Sioux and the Ojibwe,[7] he may have felt compelled to do something dramatic on the agreed day but did not want to risk defeat at another location while he was waiting for substantial reinforcements.

The burning of the mission was a cheap victory. The white clergy had been frightened away from the work at Gull Lake five years earlier in 1857 and had left it in the care of a native deacon, John Johnson or Emmegahbowh. The Ottawa Indian and his family had taken flight by canoe to Crow Wing and then Fort Ripley the night before the attack. Although not a long journey, two of Emmegahbowh's younger children are said to have died from the rigors of the trip.

Flush with the satisfaction of the successful completion of his act of defiance, Hole-in-the-Day was reported to have been anxious for the arrival of the Leech Lake Pillagers so he could proceed with his planned attack against the village of Crow Wing and Fort Ripley. But the leadership of the Leech Lake bands was having second thoughts. The younger warriors, eager for battle, had quickly taken the few whites in the area into captivity and proposed a public execution; however, two respected chiefs, Buffalo and Big Dog, were not so sure Hole-in-the-Day would be the eventual victor. They persuaded their braves to bring the captives to Gull Lake, reasoning that if Hole-in-the-Day had changed his mind or had not been successful, the Leech Lake Indians would be left alone to feel the wrath of the whites. After a two-day journey, they arrived at the appointed rendezvous between Round Lake and Gull Lake. Here they found Hole-in-the-Day less sure of his plan and the captives were eventually released.

Several things had happened. When Deacon Emmegahbowh and his family reached Crow Wing and Fort Ripley, panic was the natural reaction. Major Walker, Indian Agent near the village, took off alone for St. Paul; he was later found dead along the trail. It is believed that he committed suicide near Monticello. Other whites and mixed bloods pleaded with the Indians of the area not to join the uprising. Clement Beaulieu, the trading post operator (who was highly respected by Hole-in-the-Day), and George Sweet of the then tiny village of St. Cloud made a direct appeal to the chief. Father Pierz courageously entered the armed camp and con-

St. Columba Indian Mission of Gull Lake, sketched in 1852. It was Hole-in-the-Day's first target.

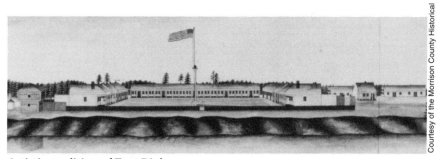

Artist's rendition of Fort Ripley.

Courtesy of the Crow Wing County Historical Society.

Oua-wi-sain-shish (Bad Boy). He may have been "Bad Boy" to Hole-in-the-Day but he was a hero to the whites of central Minnesota.

fronted the leadership head-on. Another hero—and perhaps the most effective in dissuading the Ojibwe from continuing on the warpath—was Chief Bad Boy of Mille Lacs Lake. He had left Gull Lake a few years before in a spirit of deep resentment because Hole-in-the-Day had been recognized by the white government as head chief of the area. Ironically, it was now the chief who had been passed over by the whites who helped save the lives of scores of white settlers. Bad Boy and the other Mille Lacs chiefs marched on Fort Ripley—not to wage war as was first thought by the panic-stricken settlers—but rather to offer their support and, if necessary, even to join in battle against Hole-in-the-Day. Further, he sent a messenger directly to the Gull Lake chieftain advising him of his decision. Hole-in-the-Day may have been a lot of things, but he was not stupid. Reluctantly he permitted the abortion of the campaign.

The Blueberry War

The city of Brainerd was founded in 1870 by the Northern Pacific Railroad at the point where the tracks crossed the Mississippi River (on the east side).

The Blueberry War of 1872 brought a great deal of excitement to the frontier town. In July of that year, the twenty-year-old daughter of David McArthur was sent on an errand to Crow Wing. When she did not return, a search party was organized. Although she was not found, rumors spread that two half-breeds had attacked and murdered her. Under interrogation, the suspects confessed and led authorities to a place where her body had been burned. They were promptly imprisoned in the local jail, a structure made of wood. A mob estimated at 300 people broke into the jail and took the prisoners to the Last Turn Saloon and prepared to hang them from a tall pine tree in front of the tavern. The first was quickly hung, but as the second was being "strung up," he freed his hands, grabbed the rope above his head, and scrambled up onto the branch over which the rope had been thrown. Several shots were fired from below and the half-breed was killed. People farther back in the crowd could not see what was happening and assumed Indians had come to the rescue. Most fled in pandemonium!

Still fearing Indian reprisals, soldiers were summoned; they arrived three days later by a train.

Shortly thereafter, a fleet of Indian canoes were seen coming down the Mississippi. It was assumed the town was under attack. Actually, the canoes were filled with containers of blueberries which the Indians hoped to trade! The whole episode was given the name, the Blueberry War.

Unrest Continues On The New Frontier

During the last half of the 19th century (1880s), the arrival of thousands of white immigrants in the North American Heartland resulted in grave concerns on the part of both the Indians and the whites. Because huge amounts of land were purchased by the U.S. and Canadian governments through a series of treaties, the Indian peoples were compacted into reservations. As they traveled from reservation to reservation or visited lakes and streams their ancestors had fished and hunted for generations, concerns and conflicts were inevitable.

Forts Snelling, Ripley and Ridgely had been constructed to keep peace among the tribes and to protect the whites. With the construction of Fort Ridgely on the Upper Minnesota River in 1853, there was less need for Fort Ripley and it was abandoned in July of 1857. However, no sooner had the military left than a few of the Ojibwe went on a rampage, killing a German settler near Gull Lake and burning out several others. People at the St. Columba Mission on Gull Lake captured the renegades and brought them to Fort Ripley. When they found that the soldiers were gone, they turned their prisoners over to the sheriff at the Little Falls settlement. He put them in chains and headed for Fort Snelling. An armed band of men overtook him and relieved him of his prisoners. They returned with them as far as Swan River, where they hanged them and buried them in a single grave, still handcuffed together. After this incident, the military quickly returned.

Frontier justice was often more swift than just and legal representation was rarely available to the Indians. Punishment by hanging for crimes less serious than murder were not uncommon.

Several years later, in 1884, the people of Motley expressed concern about Indians in the area in the following telegram to Governor Hubbard:

The above documents indicate that many Motley citizens were concerned about an Indian uprising in 1884. Their petition for help was sent to Governor Hubbard.

H.B. Morrison, owner of a brickyard and sawmill in Motley disagreed with those who sent the telegram and wrote the governor two days later in support of the Indian people of the area.

These are just a few examples of white-Indian conflict and concerns during the 1800s which did not escalate into major confrontations. But when taken together with the significant conflicts (Seven Oaks Massacre at Pembina in 1816; the conflict in southern Minnesota in 1862; and Leech Lake in 1898), one has a picture of substantial problems between the white settlers and the Sioux and Ojibwe Indian tribes.

The Last Of The White-Indian Wars

If one were to ask someone from one of the eastern seaboard states where the last White-Indian conflict took place in our country - few would guess "Minnesota". But it is really not so surprising when one realizes that northern Minnesota was about as undeveloped in 1898 as any of the states of the West or Southwest.

The incident which brought troops to Leech Lake was in itself quite insignificant, and if a rifle had not fallen from its stacked position and accidentally discharged, there may have been no battle at all. However, the general discontent and restlessness of the Indians at that time made the incident possible. One might also speculate that the danger of a general Indian uprising across the lake region would have been much more likely except for the knowledge all Ojibwe had of how the Sioux had been literally driven out of southern Minnesota 36 years earlier following the fighting which had taken place in the New Ulm-Mankato area.

The center of the controversy was Chief Pugona-geshig, called "Old Bug" by the whites. At the root of the problem was the illegal sale of liquor to the Indians. Government agents were seeking witnesses to convict "bootleggers" and Pugona-geshig was being sought as such a witness for a trial which was to be held in Duluth. In his younger days, the chief had been taken to this same city for a similar purpose and was allegedly left to find his own way back to Leech Lake. As the story goes, he was twice thrown off trains when he couldn't produce a ticket. It was winter, and he endured many hardships, including freezing, before returning to his home on Leech Lake. He vowed never again to be subjected to such treatment and this time he hid in the forest.

Eventually he was forced to come out of hiding to report at the old agency in Trader Bay in order to collect his regular census payment. He simply could not forego what he thought was rightfully his. U.S. Marshals promptly arrested him; when he resisted, he was handcuffed. At first, other Indians were hesitant to interfere, but his cries for help and taunting words finally shamed some of the younger braves into attacking the marshals and roughing them up. The chief made for the woods but handi-

Chief Pugona-geshig (on the left), nicknamed "Old Bug" (the Ojibwe "P" is pronounced "B"). He was the focal point of the last white-Indian war in our country.

Courtesy of the Minnesota County Historical Society.

capped by his age and the shackles, he was caught again. This time a group of Indian women got into the act and Pugona-geshig made good his escape. In the days that followed, a large number of Indians rallied to his support and the marshals, recognizing their own limitations and the gravity of the situation, requested military support.

Law and order had to be maintained and a contingent of soldiers was sent north under the leadership of General John Bacon and Major Melville C. Wilkinson. The author's father, Richard Lund, was living in Brainerd at the time; although only eight years old, he had vivid recollections of the troop trains as they pulled into that city on their way to Walker. Even though local citizens were apprehensive, they generally made light of the situation and cheered the soldiers on their way. He also recalled the somewhat relieved but very sober crowd that greeted a returning train with its dead and wounded.

The first troop train arrived in September, the second just after the first of October, and a third came later. On the morning of October 5, 1898, General Bacon, Major Wilkinson, and about two hundred soldiers set out from Walker on barges, headed for Sugar Point (now also called Battle Point) where the fugitive had his cabin home and a garden. The soldiers spent the morning searching in vain; they encountered only a few women and children. At noon, a group of men were instructed to break for lunch in a clearing by the log cabin. As they stacked their rifles, one fell and accidentally discharged. Unknown to the soldiers, there were scores of Indians hiding in the woods around the clearing. One or more of the Indians apparently assumed they had been discovered and returned fire. The soldiers took refuge in the cabin and continued the battle. By the time the Indians retreated into the oblivion of the forest, six soldiers lay dead, including Major Wilkinson (for whom the tiny village near Leech Lake on Highway 371 is named), and ten were wounded. The Indians apparently suffered no casualties although it was rumored that one had been killed. It is to the credit of the military that vengeance was not taken. The chief was allowed to make good his escape to the cabin of his brother, Chief Red Blanket, on Boy River, and peace was restored. When the citizens of the tiny village of Walker heard the shots from Sugar Point and when no one returned from the fighting to report its outcome, they feared the worst and assumed that the Indians had wiped out the military expedition. They wired the mayor of Brainerd and asked that he organize what amounted to a citizens' militia to help them. Mayor Nevers responded and a special train left Brainerd for Walker. Dr. James Camp[8] was among those who volunteered.

Pauline Wold,[9] who worked for Dr. Camp, wrote the following account of Brainerd's reaction to the uprising:

"Leech Lake was only sixty miles away, and Indians on the warpath might easily reach us! And with all our men and guns gone, we felt very much like "babes in the woods."

"Few people in Brainerd slept much that night. The next day we tried to get into communication with Walker, but the wires had evidently been cut, and no trains were running. The second day wild rumors were abroad that Indians on their ponies had rushed through town, but there was no news from Walker. On the morning of the third day Mrs. Nevers[10] called to find out if we had heard anything at the hospital, but we had not. She said she had heard that there had been a battle and that several men from Brainerd had been injured or killed, among them, Dr. Camp. Not very good news for us! We were all feeling pretty "jittery." On the following morning a wire reached the hospital asking us to meet a train coming down that morning, and to bring soup, hot coffee, and surgical dressing. I must admit we were rather an excited crowd at the station. With sinking hearts we noticed as the train pulled in that there were several rough pine boxes in the baggage car. A shudder went through me when I thought that perhaps Dr. Camp was in one of them! Imagine our relief when the first to get off the train were Dr. Camp and Mayor Nevers. They told us at once that all the men from Brainerd were safe.

"Not many questions were asked, as soon we were busy feeding and dressing wounded soldiers and trying to make them a little more comfortable for a trip down to Fort Snelling hospital. They told us that half a dozen soldiers had been killed, among them the beloved Major Melville C. Wilkinson, and that ten had been wounded. One of the boys had been shot through the thigh. They were indignant to think that some of them had gone through the Cuban campaign without a scratch, and here they were being killed by a handful of Indians.

"That evening we had a little party to welcome Dr. Camp. A few neighbors came in, and we then heard from him what had really

happened. Upon reaching Walker, the Brainerd men found every-
thing in great commotion and everyone scared to death. They heard
that the soldiers, eighty of them under the command of General
John M. Bacon and Major Wilkinson, had gone to Sugar Point near
Bear Island in the morning, as news had reached them that 'Old
Bug' had been seen there. At Walker a lot of shooting had been heard
during the day, but no one had returned to tell what was happening.
It was feared that the Indians were getting the best of it.

    "As Dr. Camp had spent a couple of years as the resident physician
at Fort Totten, the men elected him their leader, thinking that per-

Courtesy of the Cass County Historical Society.

The village of Cass Lake was worried, too. This fortification was still standing
two or three years after the battle when this picture was taken.

haps he knew more about handling Indians than they did. So the
first thing he did was to gather all the women and children into the
Walker Hotel, the only brick building in town. Next he placed guards
on all the roads leading into town. 'I knew this was a very fooling
precaution,' said Dr. Camp, 'for if the Indians wanted to come they
would use their own trails that nobody else knew, and they would
not use the beaten highways. But I did this to let people know that
something was being done. I thought it might act as a nerve sedative
- something they needed very badly just then.'

"The Brainerd group talked things over during the night and decided to cross the lake as soon as daybreak came and find out what was happening. Early the next morning they got a large barge and also some cordwood, which they piled in the center as a barricade to hide behind in case of need.

"At the 'Narrows' before entering the big lake, the party found a band of Indians, headed by Chief Flatmouth.[11] They called and asked, 'Where are you going?' The men answered , 'Over to Sugar Point to see what is happening over there,'" and the Indians replied, 'We will be here when you come back.'

"When the barge neared the point, the men went ahead very cautiously, not knowing what might be coming. Everything seemed very quiet, with only a few men running down to the beach. They seemed to be in soldiers' uniforms, but that could be a disguise and they might be Indians. The newcomers beached their boat very carefully and went behind the barricade in case they should be shot at. To their relief, however, they were greeted by soldiers and a couple of newspaper reporters who had gone along to write up the happenings at Leech Lake. A couple of more frightened men were never seen. They climbed aboard like two little monkeys and swiftly hid behind the barricade.'

"Of course, by this time the action was over and the reporters had nothing to fear,"

And so ended the last of the "Indian Wars"!

During the 1800s, the killing of hundreds of whites led the settlers to mistrust and even hate the Indian peoples. On the other hand, late and meager treaty payments, compression into reservations, the 25¢ bounty on Sioux scalps and frontier justice — including hangings sometimes without trial — resulted in mistrust and hatred by the Indian peoples of the whites.

With this history of conflict and mutual mistrust it is little wonder problems exist to this day.

[1] For further information about the fur trade rivalries, consult *Lake Superior Yesterday and Today* by this author.

[2] Dickson traded up and down the Mississippi and had major posts on Leech and Sandy Lakes.

[3] For example, the Winnebago Sioux of Iowa were moved as a tribe to the Long Prairie area to make room for settlers. For further details, see *"Our Historic Upper Mississippi"* by this author.

[4] This may have been the same person identified as "Bad Hail" in the previous chapter.

[5] A North Dakota fort on the west side of the Red River.

[6] Some accounts say that he was picking berries.

[7] Historians do not agree whether or not there was collaboration between these age-old rival tribes, but there is some circumstantial evidence that Chiefs Little Crow and Hole-in-the-Day conspired. At any rate, on the very same day, August 18, 1862, the Sioux and the Ojibway swung into action more than one hundred miles apart. The simultaneous attacks, according to historian Carl Zapffe, were supposedly timed for the middle of the day of the three-day dark of the moon period which occurs monthly - when there is no moon at all, all night long. We do know that the Dakota Sioux and the Ojibwe (including Hole-in-the-Day and Little Crow) had been together shortly before this at Fort Snelling. It was customary for Indian peoples to use the dark of the moon as a time to start journeys, etc.

[8] Dr. Camp was a highly respected and well-liked pioneer physician in Brainerd. He also owned a cabin near the thoroughfare between the Upper and Lower Mission Lakes. A "pothole" between the lakes and the Mississippi River is named for him. The author's father recalled that the doctor's well-trained horse would allow Camp to shoot partridges and other game from the buggy and would patiently wait while he retrieved them or gave chase.

[9] Wold, Pauline, *Some Recollections of the Leech Lake Uprising*, Minnesota History, 1943.

[10] The wife of the mayor of Brainerd.

[11] Chief Flatmouth II, son of the legendary chief of the Pillagers of the first part of the century. Apparently there were many Indians who wanted no part of the uprising, nor did Pugona-geshig have the affection or respect of all Leech Lake Indians.

CHAPTER VIII

WHAT ARE THE IMPLICATIONS FOR TODAY'S PROBLEMS?

In recent years there have been efforts by Native Americans to restore hunting and fishing rights as stated in the several treaties governing the transfer of land from the tribes to the Canadian and United States governments. Some of the reasons for their demands go deeper than hunting and fishing rights. As the Ojibwe and the Dakota Sioux contemplate their own history it is not hard to find reasons for discontent with the treaty settlements. Apart from hunting and fishing rights, it is natural to wonder about the amount of the payments for what has become valuable land. Most Native Americans believe the treaties to have been unfair. One way to correct some of the perceived injustice is to make certain every promise by the government is kept. The single issue most easily addressed is hunting and fishing rights. It is also an issue that is guaranteed to receive a great deal of media attention. Looking back beyond the treaties, the Indian people are very much aware that their ancestors shed a good deal of blood in fighting other tribes for those territories, and yet, gave them up to the whites through peaceful negotiations. Land that Indian peoples had paid for with their blood was procured by and for non-Indians through their governments for relatively little cash with little or no personal hardship or sacrifice. For the Native Americans there is also a basic issue of respect - respect for the treaties and respect for the Indian people.

The following are examples taken from three treaties. As you read them you can make your own conclusion as to relative fairness and justice or whether it made sense to try to make farmers out of a hunting, fishing and gathering culture.

This is an excerpt from the 1866 Treaty between the U.S. Government and the Nett Lake Bands, creating the Nett Lake Reservation:

The United States agrees to erect, on the Nett Lake reserve, the following named buildings: one blacksmith shop, to cost not exceeding five hundred dollars; one schoolhouse, to cost not exceeding five hundred dollars; and eight houses for their chiefs, to cost not exceeding four hundred dollars each; and a building for an agency house and store-house to cost not exceeding two thousand dollars.

Also for the support of the blacksmith and his outfit, fifteen hundred dollars annually, for twenty years; for school purposes eight hundred dollars; for farming tools and instruction in farming, eight hundred dollars; for annuity payment, eleven thousand dollars, partly in cash and partly in goods.

Also thirty thousand dollars for presents to the chiefs and to the people upon the ratification of this treaty; and not to exceed ten thousand dollars for the expenses of transportation and subsistence of the Indian delegates who visited Washington for the purpose of negotiating this treaty.

The following is the Treaty of 1873 between the Canadian Dominion government (under the Queen of England) and the Native Americans of the Lake of the Woods, the Canadian Boundary Waters and other parts of northwestern Ontario.

TREATY No. 3

ARTICLES OF A TREATY made and concluded this third day of October, in the year of Our Lord one thousand eight hundred and seventy-three, between Her Most Gracious Majesty the Queen of Great Britain and Ireland, by Her Commissioners, the Honourable Alexander Morris, Lieutenant-Governor of the Province of Manitoba and the North-west Territories; Joseph Alfred Norbert Provencher and Simon James Dawson, of the one part, and the Saulteaux Tribe of the Ojibway Indians, inhabitants of the country within the limits hereinafter defined and described, by their Chiefs chosen and named as hereinafter mentioned, of the other part.

Whereas the Indians inhabiting the said country have, pursuant to an appointment made by the said Commissioners, been convened at a meeting at the north-west angle of the Lake of the Woods to deliberate upon certain matters of interest to Her Most Gracious Majesty, of the one part, and the said Indians of the other.

And whereas the said Indians have been notified and informed by Her Majesty's said Commissioners that it is the desire of Her Majesty to open up for settlement, immigration and such other purposes as to Her Majesty may seem meet, a tract of country bounded and described as hereinafter mentioned, and to obtain the consent thereto of Her Indian subjects inhabiting the said tract, and to make a treaty and arrange with them so that there may be peace and good will between them and Her Majesty and that they may know and be assured of what allowance they are to count upon and receive from Her Majesty's bounty and benevolence.

And whereas the Indians of the said tract, duly convened in council as aforesaid, and being requested by Her Majesty's said Commissioners to name certain Chiefs and Headmen, who should be authorized on their behalf to conduct such negotiations and sign any treaty to be founded thereon, and to become responsible to Her Majesty for their faithful performance by their respective bands of such obligations as shall be assumed by them, the said Indians have thereupon named the following persons for that purpose, that is to say:

KEK-TA-PAY-PI-NAIS (Rainy River.)
KITCHI-GAY-KAKE (Rainy River.)
NOTE-NA-QUA-HUNG (North-West Angle.)
NAWE-DO-PE-NESS (Rainy River.)
POW-WA-SANG (North-West Angle.)
CANDA-COM-IGO-WE-NINIE (North-West Angle.)
PAPA-SKO-GIN (Rainy River.)
MAY-NO-WAH-TAW-WAYS-KIONG (North-West Angle.)
KITCHI-NE-KA-LE-HAN (Rainy River.)
SAH-KATCH-EWAY (Lake Seul.)
MUPA-DAY-WAH-SIN (Kettle Falls.)
ME-PIE-SIES (Rainy Lake, Fort Frances.)
OOS-CON-NA-GEITH (Rainy Lake.)
WAH-SHIS-KOUCE (Eagle Lake.)
KAH-KEE-Y-ASH (Flower Lake.)
GO-BAY (Rainy Lake.)
KA-MO-TI-ASH (White Fish Lake.)
NEE-SHO-TAL (Rainy River.)

KEE-JE-G0-KAY (Rainy River.)
SHA-SHA-GANCE (Shoal Lake.)
SHAH-WIN-NA-BI-NAIS (Shoal Lake.)
AY-ASH-A-WATH (Buffalo Point.)
PAY-AH-BEE-WASH (White Fish Bay.)
KAH-TAY-TAY-PA-E-CUTCH (Lake of the Woods.)

And thereupon, in open council, the different bands having presented their Chiefs to the said Commissioners as the Chiefs and Headmen for the purposes aforesaid of the respective bands of Indians inhabiting the said district hereinafter described:

And whereas the said Commissioners then and there received and acknowledged the persons so presented as Chiefs and Headmen for the purpose aforesaid of the respective bands of Indians inhabiting the said district hereinafter described;

And whereas the said Commissioners have proceeded to negotiate a treaty with the said Indians, and the same has been finally agreed upon and concluded, as follows, that is to say:—

The Saulteaux Tribe of the Ojibbeway Indians and all other the Indians inhabiting the district hereinafter described and defined, do hereby cede, release, surrender and yield up to the Government of the Dominion of Canada for Her Majesty the Queen and Her successors forever, all their rights, titles and privileges whatsoever, to the lands included within the following limits, that is to say:—

Commencing at a point on the Pigeon River route where the international boundary line between the Territories of Great Britain and the United States intersects the height of land separating the waters running to Lake Superior from those flowing to Lake Winnipeg; thence northerly, westerly and easterly along the height of land aforesaid, following its sinuosities, whatever their course may be, to the point at which the said height of land meets the summit of the watershed from which the streams flow to Lake Nepigon; thence northerly and westerly, or whatever may be its course, along the ridge separating the waters of the Nepigon and the Winnipeg to the height of land dividing the waters of the Albany and the Winnipeg; thence westerly and north-westerly along the height of land dividing the waters flowing to Hudson's Bay by the Albany or other rivers from those running to English River and the Winnipeg to a point on the said height of land bearing north forty-five degrees east from Fort Alexander, at the mouth of the Winnipeg; thence south forty-five degrees west to Fort Alexander, at the mouth of the Winnipeg; thence southerly along the eastern bank of the Winnipeg to the mouth of White Mouth River; thence southerly by the line described as in that part forming the eastern boundary of the tract surrendered by the Chippewa and Swampy Cree tribes of Indians to Her Majesty on the third of August, one thousand eight hundred and seventy-one, namely, by White Mouth River to White Mouth Lake, and thence on a line having the general bearing of White Mouth River to the forty-ninth parallel of north latitude; thence by the forty-ninth parallel of north latitude to the Lake of the Woods, and from thence by the international boundary line to the place beginning.

The tract comprised within the lines above described, embracing an area of fifty-five thousand square miles, be the same more or less. To have and to hold the same to Her Majesty the Queen, and Her successors forever.

And Her Majesty the Queen hereby agrees and undertakes to lay aside reserves for farming lands, due respect being had to lands at present cultivated by the said Indians, and also to lay aside and reserve for the benefit of the said Indians, to be administered and dealt with for them by Her Majesty's Government of the Dominion of Canada, in such a manner as shall seem best, other reserves of land in the said territory hereby ceded, which said reserves shall be selected and set aside where it shall be deemed most convenient and advantageous for each band or bands of Indians, by the officers of the said Government appointed for that purpose, and such selection shall be so made after conference with the Indians; provided, however, that such reserves, whether for farming or other purposes, shall in no wise exceed in all one square mile for each family of five, or in that proportion for larger or smaller families; and such selections shall be made if possible during the course of next summer, or as soon thereafter as may be found practicable, it being understood, however, that if at the time of any such selection of any reserve, as aforesaid, there are any settlers within the bounds of the lands reserved by any band, Her Majesty reserves the right to deal with such settlers as She shall deem just so as not to diminish the extent of land allotted to Indians, and provided also that the aforesaid reserves of lands, or any interest or right therein or appurtenant thereto, may be sold, leased or otherwise disposed of by the said Government for the use and benefit of the said Indians, with the consent of the Indians entitled thereto first had and obtained.

And with a view to show the satisfaction of Her Majesty with the behaviour and good conduct of Her Indians She hereby, through Her Commissioners, makes them a present of twelve dollars for each man, woman and child belonging to the bands here represented, in extinguishment of all claims heretofore preferred.

And further, Her Majesty agrees to maintain schools for instructions in such reserves hereby made as to Her Government of Her Dominion of Canada may seem advisable whenever the Indians of the reserve shall desire it.

Her Majesty further agrees with Her said Indians that within the boundary of Indian reserves, until otherwise determined by Her Government of the Dominion of Canada, no intoxicating liquor shall be allowed to be introduced or sold, and all laws now in force or hereafter to be enacted to preserve Her Indian subjects inhabiting the reserves or living elsewhere within Her North-west Territories, from the evil influences of the use of intoxicating liquors, shall be strictly enforced.

Her Majesty further agrees with Her said Indians that they, the said Indians, shall have right to pursue their avocations of hunting and fishing throughout the tract surrendered as hereinbefore described, subject to such regulations as may from time to time be made by Her Government of Her Dominion of Canada, and saving and excepting such tracts as may, from time to time, be required or taken up for settlement, mining, lumbering or other purposes by Her said Government of the Dominion of Canada, or by any of the subjects thereof duly authorized therefor by the said Government.

It is further agreed between Her Majesty and Her said Indians that such sections of the reserves above indicated as may at any time be required for Public Works or buildings of what nature soever may be appropriated for that purpose by Her Majesty's Government of the Dominion of Canada, due compensation being made for the value of any improvements thereon.

And further, that Her Majesty's Commissioners shall, as soon as possible after the execution of this treaty, cause to be taken an accurate census of all the Indians inhabiting the tract above described, distributing them in families, and shall in every year ensuing the date hereof, at some period in each year to be duly notified to the Indians, and at a place or places to be appointed for that purpose within the territory ceded, pay to each Indian person the sum of five dollars per head yearly.

It is further agreed between Her Majesty and the said Indians that the sum of fifteen hundred dollars per annum shall be yearly and every year expended by Her Majesty in the purchase of ammunition and twine for nets for the use of the said Indians.

It is further agreed between Her Majesty and the said Indians that the following articles shall be supplied to any band of said Indians who are now actually cultivating the soil or who shall hereafter commence to cultivate the land, that is to say: two hoes for every family actually cultivating, also one spade per family as aforesaid, one plough for every ten families as aforesaid, five harrows for every twenty families as aforesaid, one scythe for every family as aforesaid, and also one axe and one cross-cut saw, one hand-saw, one pit-saw, the necessary files, one grind-stone, one auger for each band, and also for each Chief for the use of his band one chest of ordinary carpenter's tools; also for each band enough of wheat, barley, potatoes and oats to plant the land actually broken up for cultivation by such band; also for each band one yoke of oxen, one bull and four cows, all the aforesaid articles to be given once for all for the encouragement of the practice of agriculture among the Indians.

It is further agreed between her Majesty and the said Indians that each Chief duly recognized as such shall receive an annual salary of twenty-five dollars per annum, and each subordinate officer, not exceeding three for each band, shall receive fifteen dollars per annum; and each such Chief and subordinate officer as aforesaid shall also receive once in every three years a suitable suit of clothing; and each Chief shall receive, in recognition of the closing of the treaty, a suitable flag and medal.

And the undersigned Chiefs, on their own behalf and on behalf of all other Indians inhabiting the tract within ceded, do hereby solemnly promise and engage to strictly observe this treaty, and also to conduct and behave themselves as good and loyal subjects of Her Majesty the Queen. They promise and engage that they will in all respects obey and abide by the law, that they will maintain peace and good order between each other, and also between themselves and other tribes of Indians, and between themselves and others of Her Majesty's subjects, whether Indians or whites, now inhabiting or hereafter to inhabit any part of the said ceded tract, and that they will not molest the person or property of any inhabitants of such ceded tract, or the property of Her Majesty the Queen, or interfere with or trouble any person passing or traveling through the said tract, or any part thereof; and that they will aid and assist the officers of Her Majesty in bringing to justice and punishment any Indian offending against the stipulations of this treaty, or infringing the laws in force in the country so ceded.

IN WITNESS WHEREOF, Her Majesty's said Commissioners and the said Indian Chiefs have hereunto subscribed and set their hands at the North-West Angle of the Lake of the Woods this day and year herein first above named.

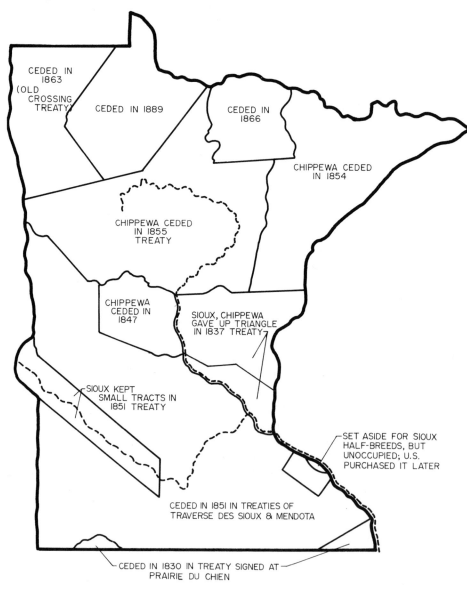

Treaties between Minnesota Indian tribes and the United States Government. (Red Lake Reserve not shown.)

TREATY WITH THE CHIPPEWA, 1837

Articles of a treaty made and concluded at St. Peters (the confluence of the St. Peters' and Mississippi rivers) in the Territory of Wisconsin.[1] between the United States of America, by their commissioner, Henry Dodge, Governor of said Territory, and the Chippewa nation of Indians, by their chiefs and headmen.

ARTICLE 1. The said Chippewa nation cede to the United States all that tract of country included within the following boundaries:

Beginning at the junction of the Crow Wing and Mississippi rivers, between twenty and thirty miles above where the Mississippi is crossed by the forty-sixth parallel of north latitude, and running thence to the north point of Lake St. Croix, one of the sources of the St. Croix river; thence to and along the dividing ridge between the waters of Lake Superior and those of the Mississippi, to the sources of the Ocha-sua-sepe a tributary of the Chippewa river; thence to a point on the Chippewa river, twenty miles below the outlet of Lake De Flambeau; thence to the junction of the Wisconsin and Pelican rivers; thence on an east course twenty-five miles; thence southerly, on a course parallel with that of the Wisconsin river, to the line dividing the territories of the Chippewa and Menomonies; thence to the Plover Portage; thence along the southern boundary of the Chippewa country, to the commencement of the boundary line dividing it from that of the Sioux, half a days march below the falls on the Chippewa river; thence with said boundary line to the mouth of Wah-tap river, at its junction with the Mississippi; and thence up the Mississippi to the place of beginning.

ARTICLE 2. In consideration of the cession aforesaid, the United States agree to make to the Chippewa nation, annually, for the term of twenty years, from the date of the ratification of this treaty, the following payments.

1. Nine thousand five hundred dollars, to be paid in money.

2. Nineteen thousand dollars, to be delivered in goods.

3. Three thousand dollars for establishing three blacksmiths shops, supporting the blacksmiths, and furnishing them with iron and steel.

4. One thousand dollars for farmers, and for supplying them and the Indians, with implements of labor, with grain or seed; and whatever else may be necessary to enable them to carry on their agricultural pursuits.

5. Two thousand dollars in provisions.

6. Five hundred dollars in tobacco.

The provisions and tobacco to be delivered at the same time with the goods, and the money to be paid; which time or times, as well as the place or places where they are to be delivered, shall be fixed upon under the direction of the President of the United States.

The blacksmiths shops to be placed at such points in the Chippewa country as shall be designated by the Superintendent of Indian Affairs, or under his direction.

If at the expiration of one or more years the Indians should prefer to receive goods, instead of the nine thousand dollars agreed to be paid to them in money, they shall be at liberty to do so. Or, should they conclude to appropriate a portion of that annuity to the establishment and support of a school or schools among them, this shall be granted them.

ARTICLE 3. The sum of one hundred thousand dollars shall be paid by the United States, to the half-breeds of the Chippewa nation, under the direction of the President. It is the wish of the Indians that their two sub-agents Daniel P. Bushnell, and Miles M. Vineyard, superintend the distribution of this money among their half-breed relations.

ARTICLE 4. The sum of seventy thousand dollars shall be applied to the payment, by the United States, of certain claims against the Indians; of which amount twenty-eight thousand dollars shall, at their request, be paid to William A. Aitkin, twenty-five thousand to Lyman M. Warren, and the balance applied to the liquidation of other just demands against them—which they acknowledge to be the case with regard to that presented by Hercules L. Dousman, for the sum of five thousand dollars: and they request that it be paid.

ARTICLE 5. The privilege of hunting, fishing, and gathering the wild rice, upon the lands, the rivers and the lakes included in the territory ceded, is guaranteed to the Indians, during the pleasure of the President of the United States.[2]

ARTICLE 6. This treaty shall be obligatory from and after its ratification by the President and Senate of the United States.

Done at St. Peters in the Territory of Wisconsin the twenty-ninth day of July eighteen hundred and thirty-seven.

Henry Dodge, Commissioner.

From Leech lake:
> Aish-ke-bo-ge-koshe, or Flat Mouth,
> R-che-o-sau-ya, or the Elder Brother.
>
> Chiefs.

> Pe-zhe-kins, the Young Buffalo,
> Ma-ghe-ga-bo, or La Trappe,
> O-be-gwa-dans, the Chief of the Earth,
> Wa-bose, or the Rabbit,
> Che-a-na-quod, or the Big Cloud.
>
> Warriors.

From Gull lake and Swan river:
> Pa-goo-na-kee-zhig, or the Hole in the Day,
> Songa-ko-mig, or the Strong Ground.
>
> Chiefs.

> Wa-boo-jig, or the White Fisher,
> Ma-cou-da, or the Bear's Heart.
>
> Warriors.

From St. Croix river:
> Pe-zhe-ke, or the Buffalo,
> Ka-be-ma-be, or the Wet Month.
>
> Chiefs.

> Pa-ga-we-we-wetung, Coming Home Hollowing,
> Ya-banse, or the Young Buck,
> Kis-ke-ta-wak, or the Cut Ear.
>
> Warriors.

From Lake Courteoville:
> Pa-qua-a-mo, or the Wood Pecker.
>
> Chief.

From Lac De Flambeau:
> Pish-ka-ga-ghe, or the White Crow,
> Na-wa-ge-wa, or the Knee,
> O-ge-ma-ga, or the Dandy,
> Pa-se-quam-jis, or the Commissioner,
> Wa-be-ne-me, or the White Thunder.
>
> Chiefs.

From La Pointe, (on Lake Superior):
    Pe-zhe-ke, or the Buffalo,
    Ta-qua-ga-na, or Two Lodges Meeting,
    Cha-che-que-o.

                               Chiefs.

From Mille Lac:
    Wa-shask-ko-kone, or Rats Liver,
    Wen-ghe-ge-she-guk, or the First Day.

                               Chiefs.

    Ada-we-ge-shik, or Both Ends of the Sky,
    Ka-ka-quap, or the Sparrow.

                             Warriors.

From Sandy Lake:
    Ka-nan-da-wa-win-zo, or Le Brocheux,
    We-we-shan-shis, the Bad Boy, or Big Mouth,
    Ke-che-wa-me-te-go, or the Big Frenchman.

                               Chiefs.

    Na-ta-me-ga-bo, the Man that stands First,
    Sa-ga-ta-gun, or Spunk.

                             Warriors.

From Snake river:
    Naudin, or the Wind,
    Sha-go-bai, or the Little Six,
    Pay-ajik, or the Lone Man,
    Na-qua-na-bie, or the Feather.

                               Chiefs.

    Ha-tau-wa,
    Wa-me-te-go-zhins, the Little Frenchman,
    Sho-ne-a, or Silver.

                             Warriors.

From Fond du Lac, (on Lake Superior):
    Mang-go-sit, or the Loons Foot,
    Shing-go-be, or the Spruce.

                               Chiefs.

From Red Cedar lake:
Mont-so-mo, or the Murdering Yell.

From Red lake:
Francois Goumean (a half breed).

From Leech lake:
Sha-wa-ghe-zhig, or the Sounding Sky,
Wa-zau-ko-ni-a, or Yellow Robe.
Warriors.

Signed in presence of—
Verplanck Van Antwerp,
   Secretary to the Commissioner.
M.M. Vineyard, U.S. Sub-Indian Agent.
Daniel P. Bushnell.
Law, Taliaferro, Indian Agent at St. Peters.
Martin Scott, Captain, Fifth Regiment Infantry.
J. Emerson, Assistant Surgeon, U.S. Army.
H.H. Sibley.
H.L. Dousman.
S.C. Stambaugh.
E. Lockwood.
Lyman M. Warren.
J.N. Nicollet.
Harmen Van Antwerp.
Wm. H. Forbes.
Jean Baptiste Dubay, Interpreter.
Peter Quinn, Interpreter.
S. Campbell, U.S. Interpreter.
Stephen Bonga, Interpreter.
Wm. W. Coriell.

(To the Indian names are subjoined a mark and seal.)

Much has been written by white man about the acquisition of Indian territories, but here is an Indian point of view of how our continent's first residents may have felt about the coming of the whites - as expressed by Lolita Taylor, a Wisconsin Ojibwe in her book, *The Native American:*[3]

"Before the signing of the Treaty of 1837 the Ojibwa were told and distinctly understood they would retain possession of their land - that the Government wanted only the mineral rights and the pine. The people were to remain on the land as long as they behaved themselves and caused no trouble. They never knew that they had ceded away their land until told to move in 1849. Now they were to leave their homes and the graves of their loved ones and go to a reservation. "Who has been misbehaving?" they asked and even traveled around to see if they could find anyone who had been causing trouble.

Older Indians were beginning to see what was happening at last. "They are as thick as the trees in the forest" they said. "They are killing our game, they are destroying the home of the deer and the bear." They shook their heads in despair as they saw the logs tearing the rice beds out of the rivers. "It won't be long before rice goes the way of the pine trees," they said. It was truly spoken. Farmers anxious to get their plows into the ground often burned off large tracts of ground to clear it for fields. Hills that should never have been cut over were left bare to erode in the wind and rain. Cattle grazed on the river banks and along the sparkling trout streams sending dirt and filth into the waters and taking away the natural cover to let rains wash silt down the banks.

To an outsider this may have seemed a bit extreme, but to the Ojibwa it was a real blow. Yet he must bow to the intruder. In many cases it was the policy of the land owner (now the white man) to complain of his Indian neighbor simply to have him removed. Land grabbers came into the country and misrepresented their rights by saying they had title to swamp lands or to land set aside for schools. In this way they gained control of much of the cranberry beds. Where railroad companies paid for the right of way through the white man's land, they simply disregarded the Indian's. Records say "they are squatters." Yes they were squatters on their own land.

Gradually the Ojibwa's life began to change. He no longer could be a logger - there were no more logs to float down the streams. His sources of food were yielding less and less. No longer could he depend on his furs, since he was subject to the white man's conservation laws that prohibited him from trapping except at certain times. Where he had once felt rich and secure in the gifts of the Great Spirit he now became insecure. And he began to distrust not only the culture that had done this to him, but his own way of life.

The Priest gave him to understand that he was living a life of sin. What had become of all the gentle ones he had known before? Were they damned because the Priest had been too late to save them? What had happened to the proud ancestors and their island sanctuary?

The educator told him he was ignorant. Not only that, his parents were ignorant, too. They were talking the wrong language, they were wearing the wrong kinds of clothes. Never mind that the European came to this country bathless - the Indian was the one called dirty.

The farmer and the industrialist called him lazy. They just couldn't understand why the Indian wasn't out to get all the money for himself. They had no idea of sharing as the Ojibwa did.

His land had been taken because it was valuable to the Europeans. So were his forests, his furs, wild rice and game. How much more could a being endure?"

What is the non-Indian's reply? The following are arguments made by non-Indians at meetings held in 1993-94 relative to fishing privileges[4] for Native Americans on Mille Lacs and other nearby Minnesota lakes:

"For their time the treaties were fair. The Indians signed voluntarily."

"They've had their pay."

"Where would the Indians be today without the other races? How would they be living - without modern health care - without modern conveniences - without formal education - without what white people have done for them?"

"The Indians have had special treatment - on and off the reservation - both financial and otherwise. Who else can get a free education or free health care?"[5]

"How much is enough?"

"They have their casinos - they have their revenge."

"So what if my ancestors ripped off somebody else's ancestors? Why should I suffer for that? If my great grandfather shot somebody else's great grandfather a hundred years ago, no one would

think of holding me responsible for harm done that man's family way back then."

"Why should the Chippewa have special rights on Mille Lacs Lake? This was originally Sioux country."

"The tribes already get a cut out of every sports license sold. They have negotiated away any special hunting for fishing privileges."

"There aren't any full-blooded Indians left. These people demanding treaty rights are as much white as red."

Author's Comment

And so the conflict goes on. No matter how the treaties are interpreted, the problems will continue until we begin looking for solutions to racial or culturally-oriented problems that will assure quality of living and equal opportunities for Indians and non-Indians alike. With continued population growth facing us on the one hand and limited geography and natural resources on the other, this will not be easy.

The use of courts to resolve problems should be only a last resort. The verdicts usually mean a win-all or lose-all solution. Wise leaders - regardless of race - are able to see conflict coming and gather together the potential adversaries to collaboratively work out strategies to address problems or issues of disagreement. The result of such insightful leadership can be a win-win situation. Sometimes, however, the best we can do is to compromise - both sides giving up something. In the real world of everyday living we know we can't have everything we want or get our way all of the time. Besides, the results can be far more lasting when everybody gives a little rather than one side winning all and the other side losing all. In a win-all / lose-all situation, even the winners will probably eventually also be losers. Human nature, being what it is, will drive the losers to seek revenge and retribution. There will be a determination to get even. Everyone will eventually be a loser to some degree.

We have seen in this book how the human history of North America's Heartland has been a very troubled history. Bloody conflict has characterized all but the last century of human relationships. During the late 1800s Native Americans stopped fighting each other and hostilities came to an end between them and the settlers. During the 1900s the Native American-white relationships became less violent but the turmoil continued and all too often the solutions were sought through win-lose strategies. Bloodshed may have finally come to an end, but economic and political conflict continue.

Haven't we matured as a civilization to a point where we can systematically help each other to meet our needs, to solve our problems and to achieve our dreams? Can't we enjoy our own culture without causing pain and loss for others?

Isn't it time that we cherish our membership in the human race more deeply than our part in a culture characterized by the color of our skins? Shouldn't our priority obligation be to all members of the human race, to our country and then to our race or culture?

Racism and prejudice continue to haunt our society. **As long as we dwell on differences - whether of color or culture - we are all fighting a losing battle.**

It is not easy to focus on commonalities rather than differences; in fact, it is extremely difficult. It is contrary to our human nature, a nature formed environmentally and maybe even genetically. By that we mean that people (granted-some more than others) have instinctive mistrust, dislike and sometimes fear of that which is different. The mistrust, dislike and fear are increased if there are differences in dearly held values - such as in religion - or if they impact us economically or affect our lifestyle. These feelings, if unattended by reason or understanding or compassion, can nurture hate, and hate, unattended, can spawn violence. What we are saying is that it is very difficult to welcome diversity. But it is an effort that can succeed; it is an effort that must be made if we are to have peaceful nations and healthy communities.

The free and open societies which we cherish in the United States and Canada protect our right to the expression of cultural practices and beliefs. This freedom sometimes exacerbates the negative emotions. When, for example, homosexuals celebrate Gay Pride Days with demonstrations and parades, gay bashing in those cities increases dramatically. When Native Americans are seen on television spearing walleyes - a practice illegal for others - prejudicial thinking and behavior by other races is increased against all Indians.

But there is hope - hope based on experience and demonstrated in recent history. For example, equality of sexes and races really has come a long way. It is hard to believe that women were not guaranteed the right to vote in the United States until the 20th century, or that slavery was practiced in that country well into the 1800s. In another example, it has only been in this generation that Protestant and Catholic Christians have come to focus on and rejoice in their common beliefs, and Christians and Jews have determined to celebrate their common values and traditions - we call it the Judeo-Christian ethic.

What has made the difference? Education? Knowledge? Understanding? Experience? Yes, all of the above. But there is something more. People, individuals, have made the difference. People of intelligence and compassion caring enough about each other to make a difference.

It is much more than just making up for the sins and wrongdoings of past generations. It is doing what is right and just and fair for today and for tomorrow.

It all begins with the individual - with you and with me. We can try to influence others - and sometimes that's appropriate - but the only behavior we are really responsible for is our own.

Social change is a slow process. It only happens when enough individuals commit themselves to a principle and then work in consort to facilitate the change needed.

In this book we have seen how Native Americans have a history of conflict among tribes. All other races have similar histories. We have also described the more recent history of white-Indian conflict. But there has been progress in relationships between the races. Surely there has been less violence. Standards of living have improved greatly for Native Americans. The governments of the United States and Canada have helped, but the Indian peoples in both countries have also pulled themselves up by their own bootstraps. Profits from casinos are making a positive difference on many reservations. Yet, racial relationships are still characterized by distrust, fear and sometimes hate. This must change. Currently it is all too often a lose-lose situation.

The author is deeply concerned that the current emphasis on cultural differences (not just Indian and white) poses a serious danger to the welfare of all, unless these differences exist under a much larger umbrella of commitment by all parties to protecting and strengthening the welfare and happiness of all peoples, regardless of culture. We must further recognize that we are Canadian or United States citizens and are more committed to that identity than to our racial or cultural identity. This is not easy to do for peoples who have suffered historically because of either nation, but it is absolutely essential that we recognize those higher obligations; otherwise, cultural loyalties will tear us apart. All we have to do is look at the bloody violence caused by putting cultural loyalties above national loyalties in such places as the former Soviet Union, South Africa, North Ireland, Rwanda, Mexico and the former Yugoslavia.

Differing cultures and races can enjoy and support each other only when we recognize that we are first of all brothers and sisters in the human race and when we acknowledge that we are Canadians or Americans, and only third - although still very important - members of a culture or race. If we continue to focus on our cultural differences instead of our commonalities we will seed conflict.

We can celebrate diversity only if we have a common higher allegiance.[6]

If our primary loyalty is to our race or culture we are focusing on that which will divide us. Conflicts will become inevitable and these conflicts will eventually lead to violence and bloodshed.

When we focus on everyone's needs, goals, problems and dreams and empower each other to deal with them successfully, we are building a foundation for nations at peace in an environment of prosperity.

The dream will become reality when individuals take responsibility for their own thinking and behavior and join with others of like mind and determine to make a difference.

Let's do it!

[1] Present-day Minnesota was a part of the Wisconsin Territory in 1837. The St. Peters River is now called "The Minnesota".

[2] President Taylor canceled these rights but they were later reinstated.

[3] Taylor, Lolita, *The Native American*, 1976.

[4] Treaty of 1837.

[5] Actually not true in all situations.

[6] That common higher allegiance may be to a country, to a religious faith, to an athletic team, etc.

Other Books by Duane R. Lund
Andrew, Youngest Lumberjack
A Beginner's Guide to Hunting and Trapping
A Kid's Guidebook to Fishing Secrets
Early Native American Recipes and Remedies
Fishing and Hunting Stories from The Lake of the Woods
Lake of the Woods, Yesterday and Today, Vol. 1
Lake of the Woods, Earliest Accounts, Vol. 2
Our Historic Boundary Waters
Our Historic Upper Mississippi
Tales of Four Lakes and a River
The Youngest Voyageur
White Indian Boy
Nature's Bounty for Your Table
The North Shore of Lake Superior, Yesterday and Today
101 Favorite Freshwater Fish Recipes
101 Favorite Wild Rice Recipes
101 Favorite Mushroom Recipes
Camp Cooking, Made Easy and Fun
Sauces, Seasonings and Marinades for Fish and Wild Game
The Scandinavian Cookbook
Gourmet Freshwater Fish Recipes, Quick and Easy
101 Ways to Add to Your Income
Traditional Holiday Ethnic Recipes - collected all over the world

About the Author
- EDUCATOR (RETIRED, SUPERINTENDENT OF SCHOOLS, STAPLES, MINNESOTA);
- HISTORIAN (PAST MEMBER OF EXECUTIVE BOARD, MINNESOTA HISTORICAL SOCIETY); Past Member of BWCA and National Wilderness Trails Advisory Committees;
- TACKLE MANUFACTURER (PRESIDENT, LUND TACKLE CO.);
- WILDLIFE ARTIST, OUTDOORSMAN.